Second BBC tv

Top of the Form Quiz Book

compiled by Boswell Taylor

The book of the international television programme which entertains while it tests the reader's knowledge of the world

A valuable reference book for the home.

Also available in Knight Books
First BBC tv Top of the Form quiz book
Third BBC tv Top of the Form quiz book
Fourth BBC tv Top of the Form quiz book
Fifth BBC tv Top of the Form quiz book

Second BBC tv
Top of the Form
Quiz Book

compiled by Boswell Taylor

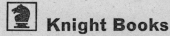

Knight Books

the paperback division of Brockhampton Press

by arrangement with the British Broadcasting Corporation

The publishers would like to express their
gratitude for all the help in the making
of this book received from the BBC
Outside Broadcasts Department.

ISBN 0 340 04246 X

First published 1969 by Knight Books,
the paperback division of Brockhampton Press Ltd, Leicester
Fifth impression 1973

Printed and bound in Great Britain by
Cox & Wyman Ltd, London, Reading and Fakenham

Text copyright © 1969 Boswell Taylor
Drawings by Leslie Marshall © 1969 Brockhampton Press Ltd

Cartoon drawings © 1969 British Broadcasting Corporation

Contents

This is the question

by Geoffrey Wheeler

Question Master
BBC tv Top of the Form

When I walked into Television Centre seven years ago for an audition for a new series to be called *Television Top of the Form*, I had no idea of the many exciting experiences and the enjoyable visits to different parts of the country that I would have in the future.

David Dimbleby and myself were the fortunate couple to be selected to act as question masters. Perhaps, before I set foot in the first school, I had the mistaken impression that all I would have to do would be to ask a number of questions and say 'right' or 'wrong'. But David and I soon learnt that there was much more to our work as question masters than that.

One of the problems is that there are three centres. The question masters are with the two schools, and there is also a central studio, often many miles away. A director and his production assistant, engineers and cameramen are with us in the school. Despite the technical complications, which are inevitable, the great advantage is that we each have an excited audience all anxious for their team to win. This gives an atmosphere to the programme that would be completely lost if the production came direct from a studio. One of the greatest difficulties at one time was to avoid a feeling of identification with the team. Carried too far it would make it impossible for the question master to award points fairly.

For me the programme begins when I receive the script and look through the questions and answers. If I feel that the team I represent has some particular difficulty, I have an opportunity to discuss it with the producer, directors, question setter and the other question master, when we meet at the briefing session. Very soon after the briefing session we travel to the schools.

I meet the team early during the morning of the programme recording. They are usually a little nervous, and one of my main aims before the programme begins is to help them to feel relaxed. We have a light-hearted rehearsal, with the other school taking part. It is always a happy moment for me to see my opposite number on the screen. For some reason the team is always amused at their opposite numbers. Then, after a short interval, the programme begins and we forget technicalities in the challenge and fun of the game.

I value the links that I have made with the schools, not only with the members of the teams, but with the head teachers and staff and the other pupils in the school. Sometimes these relationships are lasting ones. I shall for example never forget the kindness that was showered upon me by the teachers and children of a Scottish school when they heard that I had had a skiing accident in the mountains and was a patient in the local hospital.

When a series ends there is always a moment of sadness. During the last few months I have been meeting the participants and watching their progress from match to match. I have got to know the teams and react myself to their moments of anxiety and their moments of triumph. Then it's all over. But there is a consolation. In a few weeks' time another series begins, and once more I shall be packing my bag and setting out for another school. What will this team be like, I wonder!

We cross the ocean

by Dr Emmett O'Grady

*Vice-Dean of the University of Ottawa
Adjudicator for the Canadian teams
in Transworld Top Team*

I was the fortunate adult with a group of seventeen-year-old students who took part in the Canada *v* United Kingdom *Transworld Top Team* quiz programme.

Bringing the twenty-four students together from London, Glasgow and Belfast as well as Montreal, Ottawa and Toronto was a joint project of the British and Canadian Broadcasting Corporations or, more explicitly, Bill Wright of the BBC in London and of Sandy Stewart of the CBC in Toronto. Their experience, producing *Top of the Form* and *Reach for the Top* (the Canadian quiz programme) for television, led them to dream of international contests between the United Kingdom and the Canadian teams.

The organizers of the competitions had hoped that goodwill would outweigh rivalry and winning friends would matter more than winning games. Their wish came true. The ten programmes televised resulted in a very close competition, but an opportunity to visit a part of the world they had never seen and to meet young people of their own age, meant as much to the students as the games themselves.

As important as visiting one another's countries was the opportunity of getting to know fellow students from other parts of the Commonwealth. The boys and girls chosen to participate in the series of programmes were, naturally, very intelligent young people. Many were the opportunities for them to discuss their countries, the relations between them, their roles in the modern world and the period of change that we are all living through. These exchanges of views will, in the long run, far surpass in importance the contests recorded for television. It is to the credit of the organizers of the tour that such informal discussions were encouraged and that a lot of free time was made available for them.

Most of these students are on the threshold of university studies. Some of them have already been admitted by such universities as Oxford, McGill, Cambridge and Toronto. Others plan to continue their studies in other universities of the Commonwealth. It may not be too much to believe that their experience as participants in *Transworld Top Team* will have aroused an interest in international co-operation that may well give direction to their studies in the years to come.

Teilhard de Chardin, the French philosopher and scientist, once wrote:

'There is now incontrovertible evidence that mankind has just entered upon the greatest period of change the world has ever known. The ills from which we are suffering have had their seat in the very foundations of human thought. But today something is happening to the whole structure of human consciousness. A fresh kind of life is starting.'

One of these changes is sometimes called the 'information explosion' in an age of rapidly developing communication. The twenty-four students who participated in this international exchange broadened their outlook on world affairs by giving thought to the problems that perplex modern man. It is to be hoped that the BBC and CBC will continue to encourage and make possible such fruitful meetings of students from the Old and New Worlds.

Is that a fact?

by *Boswell Taylor*

Question Setter,
BBC tv Top of the Form

Inevitably there comes a time in the life of every student when he breaks out of the cosy cocoon of classroom learning and discovers that he has to find out for himself. It is then, according to our proverb pedlars, that his real education begins. He loses his mentor and he loses his ready answer book. He not only has to find out the answer, but he has first to find out the source from which to cull his information. It is this ability to find out where to get information that sorts out the students from the scholars, the men from the boys.

We all realize that education does not end with the leaving certificate but we rather expect life to set out her wares like the huckster at a market. The fact is we must work as hard to educate ourselves as our teachers worked to impart knowledge when we were at school. Fortunately this process of self-education begins long before we leave school. Fortunately also anyone who can read the English language can rest assured that most of the answers to the questions he will be asked or will ask himself can be found somewhere. The problem is where.

It is doubtful whether any serious student will find all the source books he needs within his own home, school or college. A public library is a good source of information, and many public libraries have separate reference departments where the books cannot be loaned, but where answers to queries can be found quickly. The first necessity when using a library is a working knowledge of the Dewey Decimal System of classification. The Dewey system gives a number for each subject, and this number is shown on the spine of the book. Details of which numbers belong to which subjects can be found in the catalogue of Dewey numbers.

It is not enough to know the main classifications. The ten main categories are far too general to do more than provide a lead. To make full use of the library a knowledge of the subdivisions, particularly in one's own subject, is a great advantage. Some time spent browsing along the shelves mentally registering the kind of material that is available, and where, will be repaid a hundredfold both in efficiency and time saved when quick reference is necessary.

Students will soon find that reference to the card index will probably save the manual labour of studying the books on the shelves. This is also a necessary procedure if you wish to order books that are not available at that moment on the shelves. Do not overlook the fact that some books may be elsewhere in the library and should be inquired for at the desk, and that there may be a 'Recent additions' list that may have listed the book you want.

Bibliographies and book-lists can be obtained from numerous sources. Local libraries themselves sometimes have specialized book-lists, especially covering local industries. Authoritative books usually contain a book-list. Beware of the long list of books, articles and pamphlets, many of them impossible for the average reader to procure, that may or may not have been referred to by the author of the book, but are recorded mainly to impress. The advice of a good librarian can be helpful here, and you may well find that he will extract a much better book-list from a source unknown to you.

Specialized bibliographies, some of them concerned with

improbable topics, may be obtained as published books. For example, a comprehensive bibliography of G K Chesterton, compiled by John Sullivan and published by University of London Press Ltd will supply all the references one needs to know on the famous author. One of the most famous of all bibliographies is *The Cambridge Bibliography of English Literature*, edited by F N W Bateson. The subdivisions of literature have separate sections, and the works are listed in chronological order.

The danger with most bibliographies is that they do not take account of the most recent publications. New books supply the latest information, and may even invalidate many books formerly regarded as authoritative that preceded them. Any genuine book-list will indicate the date when it was compiled. Another possibility is to obtain the National Book League's latest readers' guides. Many schools are members of this society and can obtain these book-lists, quoting the subject, from the League's headquarters at 7 Albemarle Street, London W1X 4BB. Individual membership is possible and brings additional advantages to the ready acquisition of book-lists. In fact, the League's library of books about books is one of the best in the country.

Up-to-dateness is always a problem in obtaining information from books. A book takes some time to publish and it can last a long time on the shelves after publication. In the majority of instances this does not matter, but it must always be remembered, especially in the scientific subjects, that out-of-date information can be inaccurate. Probably because a set was passed on from generation to generation like a treasured heirloom, encyclopaedia were once considered to lack up-to-date information, but a good encyclopaedia has a continuous revision programme. Perhaps the major advantage of an encyclopaedia is that it contains a full spectrum of information, everything the average person might want to know, all arranged systematically so that it only needs an elementary knowledge of the alphabet to find a reference in a moment. Every quiz addict should have an encyclopaedia, and no serious student would dream of limiting his library to an encyclopaedia.

Londoners are well blessed. In addition to the British Museum Reading Room, haunted by such historical figures as Marx, there is the Public Record Office in Holborn with a vast library of national records, and the City of London Records Office at Guildhall to supplement it with a vast collection of municipal documents which go back to 1252.

But the quiz addict will probably never wish to travel that far, even if he is a Londoner. He will want his reference books there at his elbow so that he can check the answer or find out more about the subject at once. What kind of library should he have? Here are some recommendations.

A good up-to-date encyclopaedia

Everyman's (published by Dent), *Chambers'*, *Encyclopaedia Britannica* and *World Book* are all recommended.

A good dictionary

I prefer the *Shorter Oxford English Dictionary*. The *Concise Oxford English Dictionary* is perfectly satisfactory. Some people would recommend *Webster's*, *Thorndike-Barnhart Comprehensive Desk Dictionary* or *Chambers's Twentieth Century Dictionary*.

Year Books

Whitaker's Almanack is the best. The *Daily Mail Year Book* is good. Out-of-date year books are more misleading than helpful.

Fact Books

The Guinness Book of Records (published by Guinness Superlatives)
The Dunlop Book of Facts
Pears Cyclopaedia (published by Pelham)

Sports

Wisden Cricketers' Almanac
Playfair Football Annual, Playfair Cricket Annual, Playfair Rugby Football Annual (all published by Dickens Press)
Official Rules of Sports and Games (published by Kaye)
Almanac of Sport (published by Sampson Low)

Specialist books

Dictionary of Phrase and Fable by E C Brewer (published by Cassell)
Everyman's Dictionary of Quotations and Proverbs (published by Dent)
Familiar Quotations by J Bartlett (published by Macmillan)
Teach Yourself Encyclopaedia of Dates and Events (published by English Universities Press)
Oxford Companion to Music

Atlases

The Reader's Digest Great World Atlas
Bartholomew's Survey Gazetteer of the British Isles
Webster's Geographical Dictionary
Concise Oxford Atlas

Questions

General Knowledge 1

1 In a pantomime, Buttons is your good friend. Who are you?

2 An invention began as a penny-farthing. What is it now?

3 In what country might a senorita amuse you by dancing in time to castanets?

4 In a mythological Miss World contest to whom did Paris award the prize, and what was the prize?

5 Is a *pug mill*: (i) A gymnasium where pugilists or boxers train? (ii) A machine in which clay is mixed to make pottery? (iii) A treadwheel that small dogs turned by walking on the moving steps?

6 Is *pedology*: (i) The study of soil? (ii) The study of feet? (iii) The study of children?

7 What is another name for pyrotechnics?

8 Who wrote under the pseudonym *Boz*?

9 On what river is the Aswan Dam?

10 What was the wood used for building King Solomon's Temple?

11 What is the capital of Iraq?

12 In which city is the Red Square?

13 How old is a quinquagenarian?

14 At what temperature on the Fahrenheit scale does water boil?

15 What is the world's largest city in population?

16 Who was the first man to make a solo flight across the Atlantic?

17 In what sea do European eels breed?

18 How many sides are there on ordinary dice?

19 What did Wilhelm Roentgen discover in his experiments with electricity and photographic plates?

Literature 1

20 In what book did a little girl dream of a lobster quadrille?

21 Which marooned pirate dreamt of toasted cheese?

22 In Dickens' *Christmas Carol* who was the miser who had three dreams? And who visited him in his dreams?

23 What was the nationality of Joseph Conrad and what was his job before he wrote novels?

24 What was the nationality of George Bernard Shaw, and what was his job while writing his earlier plays?

25 Who was kidnapped and taken on board the brig *Covenant*?

26 Why was the albatross hung round the neck of the Ancient Mariner?

27 A biography is the story of a person's life. What is an autobiography?

28 According to Shakespeare to whom did Julius Caesar bequeath 75 drachmas?

29 Who was the Canadian humorist who wrote *Sunshine sketches of a little town*?

30 How did John Gilpin go 'farther than he intended'?

31 Who was Don Quixote's servant?

32 Among Dickens' characters who *asked for more*, who was *very, very 'umble*, and who was always *waiting for something to turn up*?

33 Which Australian balladist was nicknamed 'Banjo'?

34 Baroness Dudevant had love affairs with Alfred de Musset the poet and Chopin the pianist. By what name is she better known?

35 Which Yorkshire librarian wrote *Room at the top*?

36 The wife of a famous explorer from New Zealand wrote *A yak for Christmas*. Who is she, and who is her husband?

The American Continent

37 What line of latitude constitutes most of the boundary between Canada and the United States?

38 What is a hobo ballad?

39 What is the famous Hollywood Bowl?

40 Besides being a five-sided figure what is the Pentagon?

41 What is a Dude Ranch?

42 What South American country takes its name from a line of latitude?

43 What bird is known as the 'Ostrich of South America'?

44 Where is Tammany Hall?

45 What is another name for the North American 'buffalo'?

46 How many states are there in the United States of America?

47 What was the name of the last state to join the United States of America?

48 Where does America keep her vast gold bullion reserves?

49 If John Bull symbolizes Britain who symbolizes the United States?

50 What did the American 'bootleggers' do?

51 Tea-parties can be times for friendly conversation: but what famous or infamous tea-party began a war?

52 What did the Montreal 'Expo-67' celebrate?

53 Name the five Great Lakes of the St. Lawrence Seaway.

54 Between which lakes are the Niagara Falls?

55 What are the two termini of the Canadian Pacific Railway?

56 Where did the Hudson's Bay Company function, and what was its merchandise?

Speed Quiz 1

How many can you get right in TWO minutes?

---

57 For what is Don Bradman famous?

58 What King of England was killed as he hunted in the New Forest?

59 What Biblical character sold his birthright for a *'mess of pottage'*?

60 What is a vintner?

61 Who was the Dutchman who sighted New Zealand in 1642?

62 Who was the New Zealand authoress of *Prelude* and *Bliss* who said 'New Zealand is in my very bones'?

63 What sport is associated with Cowes?

64 Who was the Australian author of *The Ambassador*?

65 Who was the first man to fly across the English Channel?

66 Who lives in the Vatican?

67 What do these initials stand for – O.H.M.S.?

68 Who was the first man to run a mile in under 4 minutes?

69 Who wrote about these fictional characters – the March girls?

70 In what country was Expo-70 held?

71 What was the sword of Damocles suspended by?

72 To what does the word 'arenaceous' pertain?

73 What name was given to the Chief Magistrate of the Venetian Republic?

74 To whom is the authorized version of the Bible dedicated?

75 Who was known as the Lion of the North?

76 What would you expect to find in an aviary?

Picture Quiz – 1 Sculpture

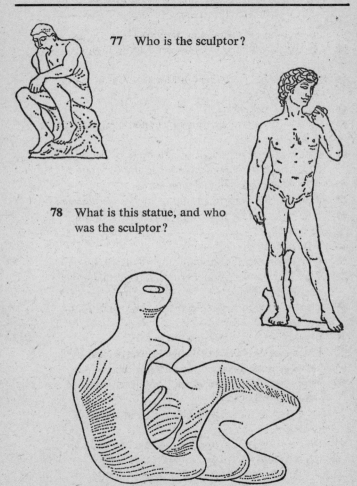

77 Who is the sculptor?

78 What is this statue, and who was the sculptor?

79 Who is the sculptor?

Team Quiz 1

80a Who were the two daughters of King Henry VIII who acceded to the throne?

81a What king called his wife 'The Flanders Mare' and who was the queen?

82a In which country did *caviar* originate?

83a Which country is noted for bird's nest soup?

84a What is a pot-boiler an author might write?

85a Which were the opposing forces at the Battle of Edge Hill?

86a What is an aquarium?

87a Explain the difference between lama and llama.

88a Why do pilgrims travel to Mecca?

89a What would you go to a *poste restante* for?

90a How would you conduct a Dutch auction?

91a Whom did John Wilkes Booth assassinate, and how?

92a What animal has a 'set' for its home?

93a What is a rodent?

94a What is a cat-call?

95a What is a 'cat's whisker'?

80b Who were the two sons of King Charles I who acceded to the throne?

81b Who was the British Prime Minister nicknamed 'Dizzy', and who was his chief political opponent?

82b In which country did spaghetti originate?

83b Which country is noted for *escargots*?

84b What is the proof that an author corrects?

85b Which were the opposing forces at the Battle of Hastings?

86b What is a planetarium?

87b Explain the difference between satire and satyr.

88b Why do pilgrims travel to Canterbury?

89b What is a *locum tenens*?

90b How would a person speak to you 'like a Dutch uncle'?

91b Whom did Charlotte Corday assassinate, and how?

92b What animal builds a dray?

93b What is a ruminant?

94b What is a 'cat-and-dog' life?

95b What is a 'cat's paw'?

Music and Song

96 How is a violin tuned?

97 In music what is the difference between sharps and flats?

98 What is an oratorio, and who was the German who lived in England for more than 40 years and wrote some of the greatest oratorios?

99 What is a madrigal?

100 There is a famous suite of music about the solar system. What is its title and the name of the composer?

101 In the song 'Molly Malone', where does she live and what does she do?

102 In which opera does the character Pooh Bah appear, and in what way is he a remarkable civil servant?

103 In what way is the music 'Overture to William Tell' concerned with the shooting of an arrow?

104 What has the 'Sleeping Beauty' ballet to do with the pricking of a finger?

105 What is a tambourine?

106 Where is Dixieland and what kind of music do you associate with it?

107 What is the next line in this chorus: 'Yankee Doodle keep it up . . .'?

108 What does Joan Baez do in the entertainment world?

109 What musical instrument did Adolphe Sax invent?

110 In an old traditional song, who went hunting with 'Ranter and Ringwood, Bellman and True'?

111 Three ladies form a singing group. The singer who hits the high notes is a soprano. What are the singers with the middle and lower compass?

112 Who composed the song 'Alexander's Ragtime Band'?

General Knowledge 2

113 What is the name of the volcano which erupted and buried Pompeii?

114 What historical assassination took place on the Ides of March?

115 Why would a twelve stone man weigh only two stones on the moon?

116 What was the ruff worn by Elizabethans?

117 What is a catacomb?

118 What is a catafalque?

119 What is a catamaran?

120 What is London's famous meat market?

121 What is a gherkin?

122 What mythological creature had one hundred eyes and never slept?

123 What mythological creature had only one eye, and that was in the middle of his forehead?

124 What does UNESCO stand for?

125 What do we mean when we use the phrase 'take French leave'?

126 What do we mean when we refer to 'castles in Spain'?

127 How many squares are there on a chess board?

128 What are the 'chinook' of Canada and the 'brickfielder' of Australia?

129 What kind of painting is 'still life'?

130 What famous family lived at Haworth Parsonage?

131 Who is the patron saint of children?

132 Who was the French explorer whose name was given to a tropical plant?

Nature

133 In nature study, what are scavengers?
134 What is the solar system?
135 How do most plants make their food?
136 What kind of a horse is a roan?
137 What is the chief feature of the Lombardy poplar?
138 Why is it necessary to put plants in an aquarium?
139 What are the male and female of deer called?
140 What is the main diet of the swift?
141 What farm crop is susceptible to damage from the Colorado beetle?
142 From what plant do we get linseed?
143 What is the chief diet of the pelican?
144 What is the difference between antler and anther?
145 If something is described as leporine what is it supposed to be like?
146 What animal gives us mohair?
147 A quadruped is a four-footed animal. What is a palmiped?
148 What is the biggest animal in the world?
149 If the 'sire' is the male parent of a horse, what is the female parent?
150 What is the clever trick of the chameleon to escape notice?
151 What animal has earned the reputation of being the number one killer of snakes?
152 What creature had an early ancestor known as the Eohippus who was no bigger than a fox?

Speed Quiz 2

How many can you get right in TWO minutes?

---

153 What is the game at which the 'Harlem Globe-Trotters' are masterly exponents?

154 What is the standard system of weights that has the same name as an ancient city?

155 On what day of the week did Robinson Crusoe meet his future servant and companion?

156 What is the colour that in heraldry is called 'vert'?

157 What is another name for hydrophobia?

158 Who created the character of Mrs Malaprop?

159 Oliver Cromwell dissolved 'The Rump' in 1653. What was 'The Rump'?

160 Which planet has rings round it?

161 What is the diet of silkworms?

162 Who was the Archbishop of Canterbury who was responsible for the compilation of the Book of Common Prayer?

163 Who used elephants to help in transporting his army over the Alps?

164 Who began a war with the abduction of Helen of Troy?

165 In judo what is the colour of the beginner's belt?

166 Who was the national hero about whom Schiller wrote a play which Rossini turned into an opera?

167 In the story by Washington Irving for how many years did Rip Van Winkle sleep?

168 How many years are there in a decade?

169 What is a monkey puzzle?

170 The slow-worm is not a worm; what kind of animal is it?

171 How many days are there in February in a leap year?

172 If a person is a Fellow of the Royal Horticultural Society, what do you suspect he is interested in?

Places

173 Which country's capital is named after a British prime minister and soldier, and what is the name of the city?

174 Which country's capital is named after its first president, and what is the name of the city?

175 What is the Colosseum?

176 What is the Parthenon?

177 What is the capital of Malaysia?

178 Where does a Muscovite come from?

179 Paris has more than thirty bridges: over what river?

180 Napoleon was born on one island and died on another. What are the names of these two islands?

181 There are geysers in many countries but they all take their name from the daddy of them all. Which one is this and where is it?

182 Suez lies at one end of the Suez Canal. What is the name of the city at the other end?

183 'Constantinople' was often used as a test of a person's spelling ability. The city has a new name now. What is Constantinople called today?

184 Trieste is a port: on what sea?

185 What is the name of the city which has the statue of the 'Little Mermaid' set in the harbour?

186 What is the capital of Tasmania?

187 What and where is St. Kitts?

188 What is the 'Milky Way'?

189 Which is the largest country in area in the world?

190 Valletta is the capital of what country?

191 If you were born and bred on the banks of the Murrumbidgee River, what would be your nationality?

Picture Quiz 2 – Buildings

192   Where is this historic gate?

193   Where is this war memorial?

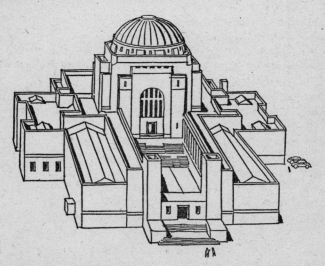

194   Where is this cathedral?

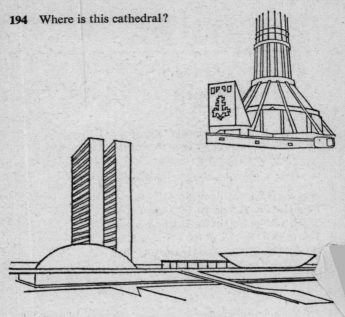

195   Where is this unusual Congress building?

196   This opera house has an unusual design. Where is it?

197 Built in the traditional French chateau style, this building is not in France. Where is it?

198 This building is shaped like an eye. Where and what is it?

199 Prisoners had their last view of liberty as they passed over this bridge. Where is it, and what suitable name has it been given?

Team Quiz 2

200a   Where do you find an oasis?
201a   What does a ventriloquist do?
202a   What is a bridle path?
203a   What is a seminar?

204a   What is a 'swan-song' and how true to nature is this
       saying?
205a   What happened to Skopje in Yugoslavia in 1963?
206a   What does 'Stop Press' mean in the newspaper world?
207a   What kind of play is a farce?

208a   What title did Beethoven give to his Symphony No 6
       in F?
209a   What have we done if we have 'let the cat out of the
       bag'?
210a   What is generally meant by the expression 'Swinging
       the lead'?
211a   Would you greet a quince, eat it, or wear it?

212a   If you had a 'mini-moke' as a pet what kind of animal
       would it be?
213a   What is the fluid or substance that is treated to
       become 'yoghourt'?
214a   If you were offered a choice between Brie, Camembert
       and Gruyere, what food would you be considering?
215a   If you have some Spode in the house, what would you
       have?

200b Where do you find an estuary?

201b What does a courier do?

202b What is a causeway?

203b What is a 'teach-in'?

204b What is the meaning of 'bee-line' and how true to nature is it?

205b What happened to the ancient city of Carthage?

206b What is a 'stop watch'?

207b What kind of play is a melodrama?

208b What name was given to Beethoven's Symphony No 9 in D minor?

209b What does this expression mean: 'to take the bull by the horns'?

210b What is a 'blind alley' job?

211b Would you greet a sari, eat it or wear it?

212b A pirate's flag was sometimes called 'The skull and crossbones'. What other name was given to it?

213b If we can have a leg of mutton, what can we have a haunch of?

214b In the culinary world what is a 'Maid of honour'?

215b If you had some Hepplewhite in your home, what would be the nature of the thing you possessed?

People of Long Ago

216   Who was the duke who routed the army of Bonnie Prince Charlie at Culloden Moor?

217   Who was crowned as emperor on Christmas Day, 800?

218   Who was the king who hid in the Isle of Athelney from his enemies?

219   What river was guarded by Spurius Lartius, Herminius and Horatius?

220   What was the misfortune that King John suffered when he visited Lincolnshire?

221   What are the two most common names of French monarchs?

222   What was the name of Shakespeare's wife?

223   What king ordered the Domesday Book to be compiled?

224   Who was the king who put his seal to Magna Carta in 1215?

225   Who was supposed to have fiddled while Rome burned?

226   What Roman emperor created Byzantium?

227   Which king was responsible for compiling an Anglo-Saxon chronicle?

228   Of which British king was it said, 'He never says a foolish thing, nor ever does a wise one'?

229   Which British king was said to be 'the wisest fool in Christendom'?

230   Who was the last Roman emperor?

231   Bloody Mary is supposed to haunt a tower. Who was she and what is the building she haunts?

232   Who were massacred in the infamous St. Bartholomew's Day Massacre?

233   Who created an empire in 1206 AD?

General Knowledge 3

234 What is the difference between slander and libel?
235 What is the difference between a tombola and a tombolo?
236 What does a meteorologist mean when he refers to 'low' in giving weather forecasts?
237 What is a tourniquet and how is it applied?
238 Of what oath are these the first words: 'I swear by Apollo, the Physician . . .'?
239 What is the 'hunting' which is done in some churches?
240 What does a cardiograph register?
241 What is the traditional name given to the log burned on a Christmas fire?
242 In street lighting two predominent colours are being used. What are they and what metallic elements are used in the tube to give these colours?
243 What were the ballistae that the Romans used to attack when they besieged a city?
244 What was the testudo – or tortoise – that the Romans used when they besieged a city?
245 What kind of weather does an anti-cyclone usually bring?
246 Complete this weather lore saying: 'A red sky at night is . . . .'
247 What kind of dramatic presentation is given at Oberammergau every ten years?
248 What would you expect to find in a phial?
249 What is the term of office of the President of the United States of America?
250 What is wrong about this statement: '*Tin Pan Alley* is a street noted for the sale of cooking utensils'?

Science

251   Why do we hear thunder after we have seen the flash of lightning?

252   What are the main chemical elements of our bones?

253   What are the chemical elements that make 'heavy water'?

254   What colour are sodium chloride and copper sulphate, and what is common to both?

255   What is the normal temperature of your body?

256   How do cavity walls help to keep a house warm during winter?

257   Why is water sometimes fluoridated?

258   Why is vinegar used for pickling?

259   Why are oranges a healthy food to eat?

260   What does a 'seismograph' record?

261   What great scientist and mathematician is linked with the Theory of Relativity?

262   What is obtained when oxygen is combined with deuterium?

263   How does a periscope work?

264   In electrical equipment why is most wire made of copper?

265   What is the name given to a 'dry' barometer?

266   What is the name given to a barometer used in aeroplanes?

267   What chemical element gets its name from the Greek word meaning 'stink'?

268   What did Watson-Watt pioneer during the Second World War?

269   What did William Harvey discover about three hundred and fifty years ago?

Sport

270   A Highland Games event is known as 'tossing the caber'. What is the 'caber'?

271   Father Brophy brought him from Ireland and sold him to Albert Williams who sold him to Mrs Arundel Kempton. He then won the St Leger, The Cesarewitch and a couple of Derbys. What was his name?

272   In what game might you be told to finish on a 'double'?

273   How many players are there in a 'curling' team or rink?

274   What County Cricket Club's ground is known as The Oval?

275   If you performed at Madison Square Garden one week and at the National Sporting Club a few weeks later what would you be and in what cities would you be performing?

276   What and where is the Cresta Run?

277   What annual race takes place between Mortlake and Putney?

278   In what game do we get cannons and pockets?

279   What game is played on a 'diamond'?

280   In what sport is 'passing the baton' an important part?

281   The Marathon race is supposed to be the same distance that a Greek ran to give the news of a victory at Marathon to the people of Athens. How far was that?

282   A toxin is a poison and a philtre is a love-potion, but what is a toxophilite?

283   What was Table Tennis called before 1921?

General Knowledge 4

284 Silver gifts are given on the twenty-fifth wedding anniversary. What should be given on fiftieth and sixtieth anniversaries?

285 What does a mahout drive?

286 A millennium is how many years?

287 What is another name for the famous picture known as the 'Mona Lisa'?

288 What do we call a young hare?

289 Complete the following:
'The best laid schemes of mice and men . . .'

290 'A friend in need . . .'

291 'You can't make a silk purse . . .'

292 What part of the body is affected in encephalitis?

293 Which countries fought in the Battle of Agincourt? Which army won and which army lost?

294 If a lighterman has nothing to do with lights, what does he do?

295 What are dovetails without feathers?

296 What is the difference between an hydrometer and an hygrometer?

297 If a cartographer does not sell postcards what does he do?

298 What was the hobby that Izaak Walton wrote a book about?

299 What was the common interest of these famous men;
Bruegel, Pietro, The Elder
Botticelli, Sandro
Cézanne, Paul

300 What were the words with which Stanley greeted David Livingstone, the missionary, when he found him?

301 Who was the first man to split the atom?

Extremes

302   What is the value of a bawbee?

303   Who was the first woman to orbit the earth?

304   What is the largest island in the world?

305   According to the Japanese, what is the mountain, the
highest in Japan, where the gods lived?

306   What was the last British possession in France?

307   In the British Isles what is the minimum number of
consecutive days with a rainfall not more than one
hundredth of an inch of rain to qualify for 'absolute
drought'?

308   What name is given to the temperature of Minus
273·15°C?

309   What is the smallest county in England?

310   What is the biggest ocean in the world?

311   What is the smallest living bird?

312   What was Laika, and in what way was it concerned in
an historic first?

313   What is Calder Hall, and in what way is it an
historic first?

314   What is the highest mountain in Scotland?

315   Special names are given to the Sunday that begins
Holy Week and the Sunday that ends it. What are they?

316   What is the first book in the Bible?

317   What is the last book in the Bible?

318   One of the smallest countries in the world is technically
under the control of the Spanish Bishop of Urgel and
the President of France. What is this country, and what
is the name of the range of mountains that surrounds it?

319   The smallest republic in the world is controlled by
two 'regent captains'. What is this country, and what
is the country that entirely surrounds it?

Games and Sport

320 What is the name given to the rules in boxing?

321 In which sport are the terms 'schussing' and 'traversing' used?

322 Where in France does an annual 24-hour race take place?

323 What is the weight of the shot in the Olympic Putting the Shot event for men?

324 All racehorses have the same official birthday. What is that?

325 What is an ace in tennis?

326 What is a scratch race?

327 In what activity does a person wear crampons and use pitons?

328 In what activity does a person wear bracers and use quivers?

329 In ice skating what numeral is the basic figure in School Figures?

330 How many players are there in a rounders team?

331 In a game of draughts how many black draughts are on the board to begin with?

332 In a game of chess how many pawns are there on the board when the game begins?

333 What is a yorker?

334 If you have a 'yarborough' in your hand what have you got?

335 Eleven teams enter a Knock-out Tournament. How many of them will get byes in the first round?

336 What is the maximum wind assistance allowed for athletics records?

337 An English cricketer who has been called 'the greatest bowler of all time' played for Staffordshire during the early nineteen hundreds. Who was he?

338 What are the names of these musical instruments?

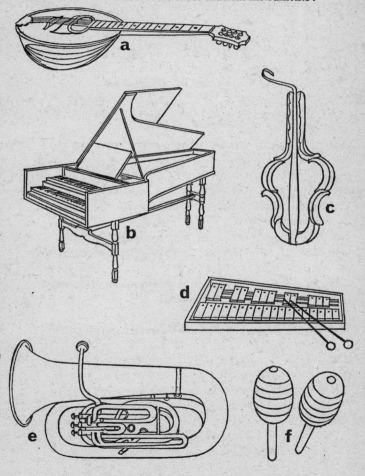

339 What are these tools or machines?

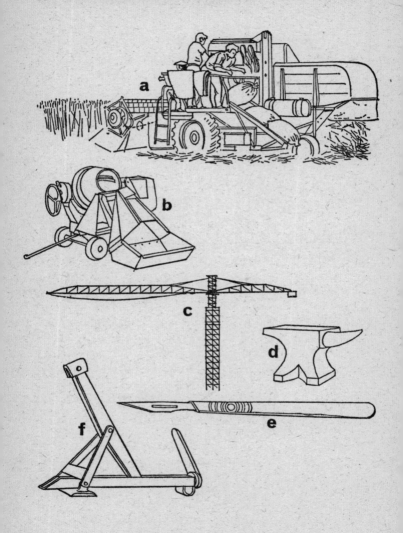

340 These are historic 'firsts'. What are they?

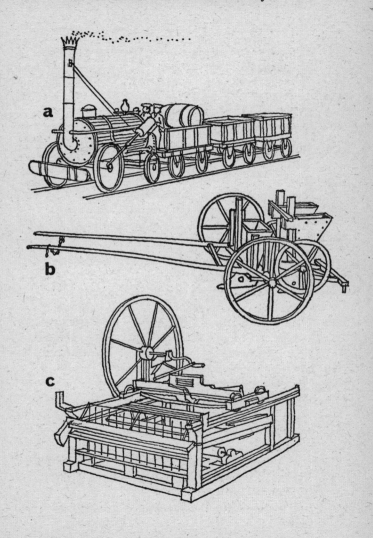

Team Quiz 3

341a With what sport or game do we associate the terms: 'Catch a crab'?

342a 'Home Plate'?

343a 'Leg glance'?

344a Who lives in the famous White House?

345a What is the nautical term which indicates the left side of a ship to a person facing the bow?

346a What is a didjeridoo?

347a If you found the 'mot juste', why would you be pleased?

348a The Bible is the sacred book of the Christians. What is the sacred book of the Muslims?

349a In geometry what do we call 'a quadrilateral whose opposite sides are parallel'?

350a Who would you expect to call out 'Pray, be upstanding . . .', and what would be happening?

351a What is the motto of the Knights of the Garter?

352a What kind of an animal was Rikki-tikki-tavi, who, in Rudyard Kipling's story, fought such a tremendous battle with a snake?

353a What book based on a true story is about Elsa the lioness in captivity?

354a If magnesium is in a firework, what happens when it burns?

355a Is a quidnunc (i) A small South American animal like a squirrel? (ii) A rich uncle? (iii) A person given to gossip?

356a In legend, who was the inquisitive Tom who got his deserts?

341b With what sport or game do we associate the terms:
'South Paw'?

342b 'Half Nelson'?

343b 'Royal Flush'?

344b Where will you find white corpuscles?

345b Where is the prow of a ship?

346b What is a tuckerbag?

347b If you copied out notes 'verbatim', what would you be doing?

348b Of which nationality is Shinto a religion?

349b In geometry what do we call 'a triangle which has two sides equal'?

350b Where and in what circumstances might these words be spoken . . . 'I spy strangers'?

351b What does the abbreviation P.S. mean?

352b In George Orwell's book *Animal Farm* who was Napoleon?

353b In what book do these three animal friends play a leading part: Mole, Ratty, and Toad?

354b If strontium nitrate is in a firework, what happens when it burns?

355b Is syntax (i) A tax on gambling? (ii) A licence paid by film companies? (iii) Sentence construction?

356b In the nursery rhyme who was Tom, the son of a performer on a musical instrument who appropriated a porcine creature?

General Knowledge 5

357 What profession or business do you associate with London's Harley Street?

358 What profession or business do you associate with London's Fleet Street?

359 What was the relationship between King Charles II and King James II of Great Britain?

360 Robert the Bruce won the Battle of Bannockburn, but who was the defeated English king?

361 What happens when our lachrymal glands are active?

362 Why might you find a 'howdah' useful if you were hunting tigers?

363 In which continent are the Atlas Mountains?

364 What name is given to a group of islands among which are St. Mary's, Tresco and Bryher?

365 What name is given to a group of islands among which are Mainland, Hoy and Flotta?

366 If a man exercised his right of franchise at an election, what would he do?

367 If you were given a 'Granny Smith', what would you have?

368 In which country do you get 'commissars'?

369 The lengths of the calendar months were fixed by the whims and fancies of Roman rulers. What determines the length of the 'lunar month'?

370 What month is named after the Roman god of doors and gates?

371 What kind of breakfast food has been named after the Roman goddess of corn and agriculture?

372 What flower that grows from a bulb is named after the legendary Greek youth who fell in love with his own reflection?

Quotations

373   What English king said these words: 'Let not poor
Nelly starve'?

374   What English queen said these words: 'I know I have
the body of a weak and feeble woman, but I have the
heart and stomach of a king . . .'?

375   The title of Hardy's book *Far from the madding
crowd* comes from a famous poem. Name the poem and
quote the next few words.

376   Who wrote a book entitled *For whom the bell tolls*
and where does the quotation come from?

377   These are lines from a famous play:
'Take up the bodies – such a sight as this becomes the
field, but here shows much amiss . . .' What is the play?

378   What woman in World War I said these words and in
what circumstances? 'Patriotism is not enough. I
must have no hatred or bitterness towards anyone.'

379   Who said these words, and when? 'Never in the field of
human conflict was so much owed by so many to so few.'

380   What is the title of the poem by Lord Tennyson which
begins:
'Half a league, half a league,
Half a league onward,
All in the valley of Death
Rode the six hundred . . .'?

381   What is the title of the poem by Lord Tennyson which
begins:
'So all day long the noise of battle roll'd
Among the mountains by the winter sea;
Until King Arthur's table, man by man,
Had fall'n in Lyonnesse about their Lord,
King Arthur . . .'?

382 Can you add the final lines to this Edward Lear limerick?
'There was an Old Man with a beard,
Who said: "It is just as I feared!
Two Owls and a Hen, . . ." '

383 If Mistress Quickly was your hostess and Francis the barman, what reply would you expect to be given if you asked him for service, and what would be the name of the tavern?

384 These words are taken from a poem in a famous book. What is the book, and who was the author?
'You are old, Father William' the young man said,
'And your hair has become very white;
And yet you incessantly stand on your head –
Do you think, at your age, it is right?'

385 What bird did Shelley call 'blithe spirit' and describe in these words:
'Higher still and higher,
From the earth thou springest
Like a cloud of fire;
The blue deep though wingest,
And singing still dost soar . . .'

386 This is an extract from a classic:
'After dinner, with my wife, to the King's house to see *The Mayden Queene*, a new play of Dryden's mightily commended for the regularity of it, and the strain and wit; and the truth is there is a comical part done by Nell, which is Florimell, that I can never hope ever to see the like done again by man or woman . . . and so to bed.'
Name the author and identify 'Nell' mentioned in the passage.

387 In one of Shakespeare's plays Puck says:
'I'll put a girdle round the earth in forty minutes.'
If Puck travelled round the Equator, how far would he have to travel in forty minutes to encircle the earth?

388 In one of Shakespeare's plays Ariel sings: 'Full
fathom five thy father lies.' How deep is that?

389 If you were standing with Captain Smollett on the
Hispaniola and you heard the following song, who
would the singers be?
'Fifteen men on the dead man's chest –
Yo-ho-ho, and a bottle of rum!
Drink and the devil had done for the rest –
Yo-ho-ho, and a bottle of rum!'

390 What is the sonnet that ends with these words:
'They also serve who only stand and wait',
and who was the poet?

391 What is the novel about the French Revolution which
begins with these words: 'It was the best of times,
it was the worst of times . . .' and who was the author?

392 This is an extract from a literary classic. What
is the title of the book and the author's name?
'Mr Bennet was so odd a mixture of quick parts,
sarcastic humour, reserve, caprice, that the
experience of three-and-twenty years had been
insufficient to make his wife understand his
character. Her mind was less difficult to develop. She
was a woman of mean understanding, little information,
and uncertain temper.'

Speed Quiz 3

How many can you get right in TWO minutes?

393   What is the name we give to the beginning of a river?

394   In Britain what is a 'Cockney'?

395   Who would you expect to see with Tweedledee?

396   If you travelled from Liverpool to Dublin, what sea would you have to cross?

397   Quills were once used as pens. From what bird were they usually taken?

398   What is the fairy-tale statue that travellers see as they enter Copenhagen harbour?

399   In which city is Wenceslaus Square?

400   If you broke a metacarpal bone, what part of your body would need treatment?

401   In pantomime, if you were Harlequin what would your partner's name be?

402   'Little Lamb, who made thee' and 'Tiger! Tiger! burning bright' are lines from two well-known poems. Who was the poet?

403   How many sisters in Chekhov's play?

404   What do we call the order of mammals that have hands and nails instead of claws?

405   Where is the famous 'La Scala' opera house?

406   Thor Heyerdahl made the voyage from Peru to Tahiti in a balsa raft. What was its name?

407   What instrument do we associate with Larry Adler?

408   The term 'stainless steel' refers to a class of steel alloys which contain a high percentage of which metal?

409   On what river are the Victoria Falls?

410   How many horsemen constitute a Polo team?

411   Where are the 'islets of Langerhans'?

Here and There

412   Of what country is Rabat the capital and Casablanca the largest city?

413   Shah Jahan built one of the most famous tombs in the world in memory of his favourite wife. What is it called?

414   With which country do we associate Marshal Tito?

415   With what country do we associate General Franco?

416   How many states are there in the United States of America?

417   What would an Irishman mean if he said that 'you had kissed the Blarney Stone'?

418   To which group of islands does Minorca belong?

419   Benito Mussolini was dictator of Italy, but what title did he take?

420   The London Underground Railway is sometimes called 'The Tube'. What is the name given to the Paris Underground Railway?

421   Where are the Cook Islands, and how did they get this name?

422   What nation used a form of writing known as hieroglyphics?

423   What was the crop that failed that caused the 'Irish Famine'?

424   On which islands do you get 'hula-hula' girls?

425   What line of latitude constitutes most of the boundary between Canada and the United States?

426   What South American country takes its name from a line of latitude?

427   Where does America keep her vast gold bullion reserves?

428   Where was the Great Trek?

Picture Quiz 4 – Costume

429   What is this headgear called?

430   What is this headgear called, and who wears it?

431   What name is given to this pouch worn in front of a Highlander's kilt?

432   Who dresses like this for special occasions?

433 This garment was worn in the 1500s.
         What is it called?

434 This hat was popular during
         the Renaissance period.
         What is it called?

435 What name is given to this cloak
         worn by the ancient Greeks?

Team Quiz 4

436a What would you expect to find in a scabbard?

437a Who lives at the Palais de l'Elysée?

438a What would you expect to find in a creel?

439a What would your profession be if you cured animals of their injuries and ailments?

440a What is a Yankee?

441a On a centigrade thermometer, what is the significance of a reading of 100°?

442a Pancake Day always falls on the same day in the week. What day is that?

443a From what plant do we obtain the drug belladonna?

444a What is the canal that links the Mediterranean and the Red Seas?

445a In the Bible what happened when Lot's wife looked back at the wicked city of Sodom?

446a Among antiques, what is a four-poster?

447a In the days of Wellington, what was a four-pounder?

448a What are the four 'voices' that take part in 'four part' singing?

449a What creature is supposed to bury its head in the sand to avoid observation by its enemies?

450a By what name is the New York stock exchange familiarly known?

451a What was the name of the ship that took the Pilgrim Fathers to the New World?

436b What would you expect to find in a quiver?

437b Who lives at Lambeth Palace?

438b What would you expect to find in a pantechnicon?

439b What would you be if you tricked a gamekeeper by snaring the pheasants and other game on his estate?

440b What is a yak?

441b On a Fahrenheit thermometer, what is the significance of 212°?

442b Ascension Day falls on the same day in the week. What day is that?

443b From what plant do we obtain the drug digitalis?

444b What is the canal that links the Atlantic and Pacific Oceans?

445b In mythology what happened if a person looked into the eyes of Medusa?

446b To a Victorian, what would a 'four-in-hand' mean?

447b To an American, why is the fourth of July a special day?

448b What are the four suits that make up a pack of playing cards?

449b Which creature is supposed to weep at the painful necessity of eating its victims?

450b By what name is the Paris stock exchange familiarly known?

451b What was the name of the ship that took Columbus to the New World?

Who am I?

To be read aloud
This is a 'Who am I?' set with facts about a person, living
or dead, historical or legendary. If you know who it is
after the first fact is given to you, you score 3 points. After
the second fact 2 points, and after the third fact 1 point.

---

452 (i) I am living in exile in Guinea, where I am
honorary president. (ii) I was Prime Minister of the
Gold Coast. (iii) I was President of Ghana from 1960 to
1966.

453 (i) I was a Russian leader who organised the Red Army.
(ii) I was born in Ukraine and died in Mexico. (iii) I
was one of the leaders of the Bolsheviks.

454 (i) I was a Gloucestershire doctor who helped to
prevent a terrible disease. (ii) I introduced vaccination.
(iii) By this means the dread disease of smallpox was
beaten.

455 (i) I was an American statesman and am also famous
for my experiments in electricity. (ii) I was an author,
printer, and publisher. (iii) I flew a kite to prove that
lightning is electricity.

456 (i) I was an author who was made a Dean of St
Patrick's in Dublin in 1713. (ii) I wrote about the
strange adventures of a shipwrecked sailor in a land of
little people. (iii) The title of my greatest work is
Gulliver's Travels.

457 (i) I was an author who was called Tusitala, Teller of
Tales, by the natives of Samoa, in the South Seas, where
I died. (ii) I was born in Scotland, and wrote a Scottish
story called *Kidnapped.* (iii) I also wrote *Treasure
Island.*

458 (i) My favourite palace was Hampton Court. (ii) Two of my advisers were sent to the block by me. (iii) I had six wives.

459 (i) I was married to Ann Hathaway. (ii) My plays were acted in the Globe. (iii) I was born and died in Stratford-upon-Avon.

460 (i) I was an Irish Antarctic explorer. (ii) I wrote *The Heart of the Antarctic* and *South*. (iii) I led a British expedition that came within 97 miles of the true South Pole in 1909.

461 (i) I was only a week old when I was proclaimed Queen. (ii) My first husband was the French Dauphin. (iii) My cousin signed my death warrant in 1587.

462 (i) I am a playwright who wrote the script for the film *Baby Doll*. (ii) I was born in Mississippi in 1914. (iii) One of my best-known plays is *Cat on a hot tin roof*.

463 (i) I made my money as a grocer and tea merchant. (ii) I opened my first grocer's shop in Glasgow in 1871 and left my money to the city for charitable purposes. (iii) As a yachtsman, I tried to win the America's Cup five times and failed each time.

464 (i) I am the drummer in a Liverpool 'pop' group. (ii) My friends are John Lennon, George Harrison and Paul McCartney. (iii) I am the fourth member of The Beatles.

465 (i) I was a military hero who worked as a candle-maker in New York and was a farmer in Italy. (ii) I fought for the unification of Italy in 1860. (iii) I commanded the 'Red Shirts'.

466 (i) After 1812 my home was at Abbotsford in Scotland. (ii) I was the anonymous author of the *Waverley* novels. (iii) Many critics believe that *The Heart of Midlothian* was my best novel.

467 (i) I was an American inventor who is famous for many inventions including the phonograph. (ii) I said that genius is 1 per cent inspiration and 99 per cent perspiration. (iii) I produced one of the first electric light bulbs and improved the telephone and the typewriter.

468 (i) I was called the 'Virgin Queen' and 'Gloriana'. (ii) My father, half-sister and half-brother reigned on the English throne before me. (iii) The Spanish Armada was defeated during my reign.

469 (i) I am a famous Australian woman singer, who made my name in *Dido and Aeneas*. (ii) In 1952 I was the principal soprano at Covent Garden. (iii) I was born in Sydney, and am one of Australia's most famous opera singers.

470 (i) I tried to establish a colony in America, which was called Virginia. (ii) While I was a prisoner in the Tower of London I wrote *The History of the World*. (iii) I am *said* to have introduced tobacco and the potato to Europe.

471 (i) I was a playwright, and one of my early plays was *Shadow of a gunman*. (ii) I was born in Dublin but exiled myself to England. (iii) One of my best-known plays is *Juno and the paycock*.

The Bible

472 What is the Pentateuch?

473 What mountain is Noah's Ark supposed to have rested on after the deluge?

474 Who was the child who was sold into slavery because he told his brothers his dreams?

475 Who was the slave who became ruler of Babylon because he told a king's dream?

476 Whose daughter was raised from the dead?

477 Who betrayed whom by cutting off his hair?

478 According to tradition, who were the three wise men?

479 And what gift did each of them bring?

480 Who was the child who was placed among the bulrushes of the Nile?

481 Who was the little boy who served God with Eli in the temple shrine?

482 The patience of Job is proverbial, and what quality is proverbially Solomon's?

483 What do we call the songs in the Bible that David is believed to have sung?

484 What do we call the stories with a moral that Jesus Christ told?

485 What mountain did Moses climb to receive the tablets containing the Ten Commandments?

486 What weapon did David use to kill Goliath, and what was the musical instrument he played to charm Saul?

487 What are cherubim and seraphim?

488 In the New Testament, who was the apostle who wrote letters to the Galatians?

489 Who was killed by whom when he was caught by his hair in an oak tree?

490 Who asked for the head of John the Baptist?

Speed Quiz 4

How many can you get right in TWO minutes?

Capitals of the world. Of which countries are these cities the capitals?

491 Budapest.

492 Quito.

493 Reykjavik.

494 Sofia.

495 Santiago.

496 Riga.

497 Tunis.

498 Addis Ababa.

499 Who were the two men of letters who had their first meeting on May 16, 1763 in a Covent Garden bookshop?

500 Name the tavern where Ben Jonson and William Shakespeare are supposed to have met their cronies.

501 If Tunku Abdul Rahman met the Lion of Judah, what two countries would be represented?

502 What is the name of the famous gate that stands just inside East Berlin?

503 What is the name given to the confederation of North German cities founded in the thirteenth century?

504 What was the elegy Shelley wrote in memory of Keats?

505 What British essayist became famous with his confessions that he was an opium-eater?

506 What name was given to the mass persecutions of the Jews in Russia at the beginning of the century?

507 What common name is often used for chloride of lime?

508 Where is the 'keel' of a ship?

509 What is the 'explosion' associated with the name of Thomas Malthus?

510 Who was the witch who called up the prophet Samuel from the grave?

General Knowledge 6

511 What was the name of the French resistance movement during World War II?

512 If you spelt a word phonetically what would you be doing?

513 In the biblical story of Noah, for how many days and nights was there continuous rainfall?

514 What is produced by the action of vinegar on copper?

515 What vicious whirlpool off the north-west coast of Norway has given its name to any dangerous whirlpool?

516 What was the Gestapo?

517 What bird does Schubert ask us to listen to with the words 'Hark! Hark!'?

518 What are the names given to the invisible waves at each end of the visible light spectrum?

519 Who is the subject of Irving Stone's fictional biography *The agony and the ecstasy*?

520 Wordsworth wrote: 'My heart leaps up when I behold'. What did he behold?

521 What acid was first obtained from 'Prussian Blue'?

522 What is the leading coffee-growing country in the world?

523 The Black Death destroyed a quarter of Europe's population. To be specific, what was the Black Death?

524 When he is not a bald man, what is a 'Mexican Hairless'?

525 What is the useful oil we get from flax?

526 What is the correct definition? An ovation is:
    (i)   Spontaneous applause (ii)   The process of laying eggs   (iii) A form of Greek transport.

527 Is pumpernickel   (i) A kind of bread?   (ii) A large yellow vegetable grown to massive proportions in South America?   (iii) A coin of little value?

528 This is a quotation from a famous speech. Who is the speaker?

'When I warned them that Britain would fight on alone whatever they did, their generals told their prime minister and his divided cabinet, "In three weeks England will have her neck wrung like a chicken." Some chicken; some neck.'

529 What was the feathered thief of Rheims?

530 If the link word between 'ornithologists' and 'owls' is 'birds', what is the link word between 'numismatists' and 'nobles'?

Literature 2

531 What was the name of Robert Browning's wife before he married her?

532 What was the name of the missionary who was the *Small Woman* in Alan Burgess's book?

533 *Carmen* is an opera. What kind of dramatic presentation is Milton's *Comus*?

534 Who created Biggles?

535 The authoress of *Adam Bede* was a Warwickshire woman. What was her pen name?

536 The author of *Three men in a boat* was a Staffordshire man. Who was he?

537 In the fairy-tale, what did Jack climb to get to the giant, and what did he run away with while the giant was sleeping?

538 In the play *Murder in the cathedral*, which was the cathedral?

539 What are the stories called that according to tradition Scheherazade told each night to keep herself alive?

540 Who was the Puritan poet who wrote *Paradise Lost*?

541 In the biography by Paul Brickhill, who was the R.A.F. pilot to *Reach for the sky*?

542 According to Chaucer, what was the name of the inn in Southwark where the Canterbury Pilgrims assembled?

543 Who was the science-fiction author who, sixty-six years ago, prophesied space travel in a book entitled *The first men in the Moon*?

544 A number of myths are told about King Midas. What was the magic gift that Dionysus gave him?

545 In fiction his friends were Athos, Porthos and Aramis. Who was he?

Team Quiz 5

546a With which country do you associate boomerangs?

547a With which country do you associate the samovar?

548a With which country do you associate the Foreign Legion?

549a If you paid your fare in yen to travel by monorail to the airport, what city would you be visiting?

550a What animal suggests porcine?

551a What bird suggests aquiline?

552a What animal suggests leonine?

553a Belgrade, the capital of Yugoslavia, lies at the junction of two rivers. The lesser one is the River Sava, but the other is much better known. What is it?

554a If a man trained at Sandhurst, what would you expect his profession to be?

555a In France who was known as the Grey Eminence?

556a Whose tomb is visited in the Hôtel des Invalides in Paris?

557a With which country do you associate *fellahin*?

558a If a toastmaster is not a chef, what is he?

559a What would you be if you carried out construction or repair work at the tops of very high buildings?

560a Who was the nursery rhyme character who fell from a wall, and even the King's horses and King's men couldn't put together again?

561a Where is the 'Abominable Snowman' supposed to live?

546b   With which country do you associate chopsticks?
547b   With which country do you associate a sauna bath?
548b   With which country do you associate the phalanx?
549b   If you shopped with roubles in the Gum, what city would you be visiting?

550b   What animal suggests ovine?
551b   What animal suggests lupine?
552b   What animal suggests bovine?
553b   Montreal lies at the junction of two rivers. One of them is the Ottawa. What is the other?

554b   What are 'au pair' girls?
555b   In Germany, who was known as the Iron Chancellor?
556b   Whose tomb is visited in the Red Square in Moscow?
557b   With which country do you associate *alpini*?

558b   If you showed a clean pair of heels you would be doing more than giving a hygiene demonstration. What would you be doing?
559b   What would you be if you performed skin grafting operations to improve a person's appearance?
560b   Who was the nursery rhyme character who fell down and broke his crown while he was on a domestic mission up a hill?
561b   Where is 'Davy Jones's Locker' supposed to be?

Picture Quiz 5 – Birds and Animals

562   What is this animal?

563   What name is given to this animal, and what is its home called?

564   What is this bird?

565   What is the diet of this creature?

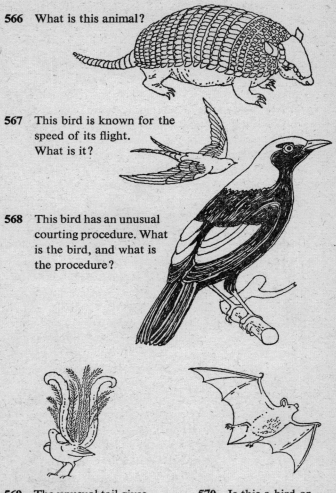

566 What is this animal?

567 This bird is known for the speed of its flight. What is it?

568 This bird has an unusual courting procedure. What is the bird, and what is the procedure?

569 The unusual tail gives this bird its name. What is it?

570 Is this a bird or a mammal?

General Knowledge 7

571 In the great movement known historically as the Reformation, what was reformed?

572 If you were given an audiometer test, what would the examiner be trying to find out?

573 What does a photometer measure?

574 In church architecture, what is a clerestory?

575 Where is the highest railway in the world?

576 Which is the longest motor car tunnel in the world?

577 In mythology, what did Atlas have to support on his shoulders?

578 The Renaissance was one of the most important periods in European history; what does the word *renaissance* mean?

579 What kind of building has a portcullis?

580 Why do you think that King James I must have been pleased that he had the Houses of Parliament searched on the night of November 4, 1605?

581 Why do you think the Trojans must have regretted taking a wooden horse into their city at the end of the siege of Troy?

582 What is the Salic Law that prevented Queen Victoria from ruling Hanover?

583 Why are silicon transistors preferred to germanium in communication equipment used in rockets?

584 Argon and helium are inert gases. What is an inert gas?

585 Pewter and bronze are alloys. What is an alloy?

586 Pointers or hands indicate the time on a watch. What indicates the time on a sundial?

587 What is the indicator in a spirit level?

588 In an historic battle Marengo was the horse that carried one general, and Copenhagen was the name of the horse which carried his enemy. What was the battle and who were the two famous generals, and which horses did they ride?

589 What is the winter solstice that occurs on December 22?

590 In what way was Tolpuddle a beginning?

591 What are the capitals of the six European Common Market countries?

592 What is the equatorial diameter of the Earth?

593 What is the equatorial circumference of the Earth?

594 In sport what are the ten events that comprise the Decathlon which are staged in the Olympic Games?

595 Why did the Romans build the Pantheon?

596 How many states are there in Australia, and what are they?

597 What are the five towns that Arnold Bennett wrote about?

598 What is the name given to the principle that states that no two electrons in an atom can occupy exactly the same position?

599 If you saw an 'orrery', what kind of thing would you be looking at?

600 What is the usual name given to the prehistoric man that Eugene Dubois called *Pithecanthropus erectus* (the apeman that walked erect)?

601 There are twelve signs of The Zodiac. What are they?

602 Magellan commanded the *Victoria* at the beginning of her voyage round the world. Who was the commander at the end of her voyage?

603 What are the names we give to rock that (i) has changed its appearance? (ii) Was once molten?

Meeting Places

604 What famous battle took place after the Congress of Vienna?

605 In what city would you be if you paid the taxi-driver in drachmas to take you to the Acropolis?

606 In what city would you be if you paid the taxi-driver in roubles to take you to the Bolshoi Theatre?

607 Where did the Allies and Germany sign the surrender agreement at the end of World War I?

608 Where did the Allies and Japan sign the surrender agreement at the end of World War II?

609 Where were the terms of the surrender at the end of the American Civil War signed?

610 Moslems always face the same direction when they pray. What is the name of the building within a mosque that they are facing?

611 If you were born and bred on the banks of the Hwang Ho, what would be your nationality?

612 Where is the famous Klondike gold field?

613 Marie Grasholtz modelled victims of the French Revolution and then set up a museum in London. By what name is she better known?

614 In Bunyan's *Pilgrim's Progress*, what is Christian's ultimate destination?

615 What are the three countries that form the European customs union known as Benelux?

616 In the story of Peter Pan, where did Peter take Wendy?

617 The Speaker presides over debates in the British House of Commons, but who presides over debates in the House of Lords?

618 In a monastery, what is the refectory used for?

619 Where was the treaty signed that began NATO?

Picture Quiz 6 – Music

620   What are these songs?

a

b

c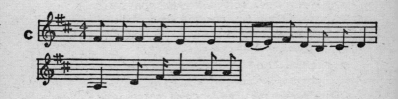

d

General Knowledge 8

621 In knitting there are two basic stitches. Plain is one of them, what is the other?

622 Dorset Blue Vinny and Double Gloucester are varieties of the same thing. What are they?

623 What do your olfactory organs help you to do?

624 You would expect to find beer in a tankard. What would you expect to find in a sarcophagus?

625 What do the rings on the Olympic Games flag represent?

626 What country ruled the Ottoman Empire?

627 A famous Russian newspaper is known as *Pravda*. What does 'pravda' mean?

628 What is meant by the Latin phrase *quod erat demonstrandum*, and in what circumstances is it used today?

629 In special circumstances in the days of Ancient Rome the Latin phrase *Morituri te salutant!* was shouted by a group of people. What is the meaning of the phrase, and what were the special circumstances?

630 What name is given to the stone that provided the key to the language of ancient Egypt?

631 What is the London borough that has given its name to the prime meridian of the world?

632 Who was the Greek woman poet that Plato called the 'Tenth Muse'?

633 What is the equation relating mass and energy that was derived from Einstein's theory of relativity?

634 What name do we give to the atomic particle which has a positive electrical charge?

635 What is the radioactive isotope that can be found in the fall-out from some nuclear bombs and which destroys the tissues that make blood?

Answers

General Knowledge 1

1 Cinderella.
2 A bicycle. The penny-farthing had one large wheel in front and a small wheel behind.
3 Spain. The castanets are small, usually wooden or ivory, instruments rattled in the hands.
4 (i) Aphrodite (ii) Apple (of Discord, marked 'To the fairest'). The disappointed goddesses were Hera and Athene.
5 (ii) A machine in which clay is mixed to make pottery.
6 (i) The study of soil.
7 Fireworks.
8 Dickens.
9 Nile.
10 Cedar (of Lebanon).
11 Baghdad.
12 Moscow.
13 Fifty.
14 212°.
15 Tokyo.
16 Charles Lindbergh.
17 Sargasso Sea.
18 Six.
19 X-rays. The use of X-rays revolutionized medical and surgical techniques, and provided new insights into the structure of the atom.

Literature 1

20 *Alice's Adventures in Wonderland.*

21 Ben Gunn in *Treasure Island* by Robert Louis Stevenson.

22 (i) (Ebenezer) Scrooge. (ii) Three ghosts: the ghosts of Christmas Past, Christmas Present, and Christmas to Come.

23 (i) Polish. (ii) Seaman or sailor or master mariner. Born Josef Teodor Konrad Korzeniowski. Born in Ukraine which was then Russian Poland. Became a master in the British Merchant Service.

24 (i) Irishman. (ii) Music and/or drama critic. Born in Dublin.

25 David Balfour (in *Kidnapped* by R. L. Stevenson).

26 Because he had shot the albatross, which in the sailors' opinion, changed their luck. (*The Lay of the Ancient Mariner* by Coleridge.)

27 A person's account of his *own* life.

28 Every Roman citizen (Act III, Sc. II).

29 Stephen Leacock.

30 John Gilpin was a fictional character whose story was told by William Cowper. John Gilpin intended to celebrate his twentieth wedding anniversary at The Bell at Edmonton. He rode on horseback while his wife travelled by chaise. The horse got out of hand and took John Gilpin on to Ware.

31 Sancho Panza.

32 (i) Oliver in *Oliver Twist*. (ii) Uriah Heep in *David Copperfield*. (iii) Mr Wilkins Micawber in *David Copperfield*.

33 Andrew Barton Paterson who wrote 'Waltzing Matilda'. Other ballads he wrote are 'The man from Snowy River' and 'Clancy of the Overflow'.

34 George Sand.

35 John Braine.

36 Lady (Louise) Hillary. Sir Edmund Hillary was the first man to ascend Mount Everest.

The American Continent

37 49°. (Sometimes referred to as the 49th parallel.)

38 A short poem or song about the life of an American tramp or migratory worker. Ballads were originally meant to be sung and they are part of the folk music of a country. They often contained a chorus or refrain. Hobo – a professional tramp.

39 A huge open-air theatre which is famous for its concerts.

40 Headquarters of the Department of Defence of the United States Government. On West bank of Potomac River in Arlington directly across from Washington. Biggest office building in the world, built in the form of a pentagon.

41 Western-style ranch which receives paying guests who want a taste of the traditional cowboy life. Some Dude Ranches are regular cattle or sheep ranches that entertain a few guests as a sideline. Other ranches are devoted entirely to the business of entertaining guests or 'dudes'.

42 Ecuador. (The Equator crosses the country and Ecuador is the Spanish for equator).

43 The rhea . . . because it looks like an ostrich.

44 New York (where Democrats' meetings are held).

45 Bison.

46 Fifty.

47 Hawaii in 1959.

48 Fort Knox.

49 Uncle Sam.

50 Smuggle alcoholic liquor, especially in the days of

American prohibition. The bottles were carried in boot legs (term dates from 1890).

51 The Boston Tea Party, in 1773. American Colonists proclaimed that there should be no taxation without representation in Parliament. To save the East India Co. from bankruptcy the tea tax was levied.
Colonists dressed as Indians tipped the tea from one ship into the Boston Harbour.

52 The 100th Anniversary of the Canadian Confederation.

53 Lakes Superior, Michigan, Huron, Erie, Ontario.

54 Lake Erie and Lake Ontario.

55 Montreal and Vancouver, British Columbia.

56 (i) Canada. (ii) Furs and skins.

Speed Quiz 1

57 His batting. He was a great Australian cricketer.

58 William Rufus, son of William the Conqueror (William II).

59 Esau the son of Isaac sold it to Jacob for a bowl of stew.

60 A wine merchant.

61 Abel Tasman, a sea captain serving with the Dutch East India Company.

62 The famous short-story writer Katherine Mansfield.

63 Yachting.

64 Morris West.

65 Bleriot.

66 The Pope.

67 On Her Majesty's Service.

68 Roger Bannister.

69 Louisa M. Alcott.

70 Japan. Osaka.

71 A single horse hair. To teach Damocles, the flatterer, a lesson, Dionusius invited him to a feast and

suspended a sword above his head. This represented the constant danger that accompanied the apparent prosperity.

72 Sand.

73 The Doge.

74 King James I of England: King James VI of Scotland.

75 Gustavus Adolphus of Sweden.

76 Birds.

Picture Quiz 1—Sculpture

77 Rodin: 'The Thinker'.

78 'David': Michelangelo.

79 Henry Moore.

Team Quiz 1

80a (i) Mary I. (ii) Elizabeth I.

80b (i) Charles II. (ii) James II.

81a (i) Henry VIII. (ii) Anne of Cleves. She was the German princess recommended by Thomas Cromwell. He was beheaded (this was a part of the reason for his execution) and Anne was divorced.

81b (i) Disraeli. (ii) Gladstone.

82a Russia. Sturgeons' roe pickled and eaten as a relish.

82b Italy. Made with flour, salt, oil and water. Paste made into strings.

83a China.

83b France (Snails).

84a Work of no literary merit written for the sake of the money it will bring in.

84b Trial impression taken from type of his book on which corrections can be made before the final printing of the book.

85a Cavaliers and Roundheads.

85b Normans and Saxons.

86a A tank or pond for keeping water animals or plants.

86b Apparatus that shows the movements of the sun, moon, planets and stars by projecting lights on the inside of a dome.

87a Lama – Tibetan or Mongolian Buddhist priest.
Llama – South American animal like the camel, but smaller, humpless and woolly haired. (Occasionally spelt with one l. Sometimes used to describe material made from its wool.)

87b Satire – composition in verse or prose holding up vice or folly to ridicule and lampooning individuals.
Satyr – Greek woodland deity in human form with horse's ears and tail. Sometimes represented goat's ears, tail, legs and budding horns. (Lusty male.)

88a Mohammed, the founder of the Islamic religion, was born in Mecca.

88b They go to the tomb of St Thomas a' Becket who had been murdered in the Cathedral.

89a Letters. This is a department of a Post Office where letters are held until called for.

89b A substitute who acts in another's absence, e.g. doctor or clergyman.

90a An auction in which the goods are at decreasing prices, the first to accept getting the goods. This is the complete reverse of the normal auction.

90b Speaking very sharply. Correcting a person very fiercely.

91a Abraham Lincoln. He rushed on to the stage after shooting Lincoln from the back of the presidential box at Ford's Theatre in Washington, America.

91b Marat, one of the leaders in the French Revolution. She stabbed him with a kitchen knife while he was in his bath.

92a Badger.

92b   Squirrel.

93a   An animal that gnaws. It has strong incisors but no canine teeth.

93b   An animal that chews the cud.

94a   A shrill whistle expressing disapproval (especially at a performance in a theatre).

94b   A life full of quarrels.

95a   An adjustable wire in a crystal wireless receiver. (The phrase 'cat's whiskers', a variant of 'cat's pyjamas', is always used in the plural but presumably is not incorrect in the singular).

95b   Person used as a tool by another. (Rarely: slight breeze rippling water in places.)

Music and Song

96   The tension of the violin string is corrected to give the right note. The sound depends upon the vibrations. The key adjusts the tension of the string so that it gives the right vibrations when it is stroked by the bow.

97   Sharp raises or sharpens a note a semi-tone; flat lowers or flattens a note a semi-tone.

98   (i) Musical composition using soloists, chorus and orchestra. No scenery or action. Subject usually biblical.   (ii) Handel, George Frederick. Lived in England for almost fifty years but born in Germany. Composed more than thirty-two oratorios including 'The Messiah'. Oratorio is named after oratory of St. Philip Neri in Rome where sacred music performances were held between 1571 and 1594.

99   A part-song for several voices. Usually has no instrumental accompaniment. Two or more voices sing separate melodies to a simple text. Extremely popular in England in the 16th Century. Composers included

William Byrd, Thomas Morely, Thomas Weelkes and John Wilbye.

100 (i) 'The Planets Suite'. (ii) Gustav Holst.

101 (i) In Dublin's fair city. (ii) Sells cockles and mussels or wheels her wheelbarrow through streets broad and narrow.

102 (i) The Mikado. (ii) He was Lord High Everything Else, and held a remarkable number of appointments.

103 William Tell, the Swiss liberator, shot an apple off his son's head.

104 The princess falls asleep when she pricks her finger with a needle and is awakened by the prince with a kiss.

105 A percussion instrument. Wooden ring with parchment head and small round metal plates called jingles. The player taps the head with knuckles or draws his fingers across the parchment, and shakes the tambourine to make the jingles ring continuously.

106 (i) The southern States of America. (ii) Jazz music – originating in New Orleans. Origin of Dixieland is disputed. One story says it has its origin in the 10 dollar bill printed in New Orleans before the Civil War. The French word *Dix* was printed on the back. Possibly from the name of a prosperous slave owner called Dixie.

107 'Yankee Doodle Dandy'.

108 She sings folk songs.

109 The saxophone. He was a Belgian instrument-maker who at the time (about 1840) was trying to improve the clarinet. He was named Antoine Joseph Sax but was known as Adolphe.

110 John Peel.

111 (i) Mezzo-soprano. (ii) Contralto.

112 Irving Berlin.

General Knowledge 2

113 Vesuvius, in A.D. 79.

114 The assassination of Julius Caesar. In the ancient
Roman Calendar 'the Ides' were the 15th of March,
July, May and October, and the 13th of the other months.

115 The Moon has only a weak surface gravity, which is one
sixth as strong as earth's surface gravity.

116 Stiffened frill worn round the neck. Several folds of
linen or muslin, cambric, holland lawn, etc.,
starched and separately goffered, worn round the neck.
Sometimes supported by a wire frame.

117 Subterranean cemetery. Originally under basilica of
St. Sebastian near Rome. Many Roman subterranean
galleries with recesses for tombs extended to similar
works elsewhere. Sometimes 'wine-cellar'.

118 Decorated stage for coffin or effigy of distinguished
person during funeral service (open hearse).

119 Boat with twin hulls side by side. *Also* – a kind of raft
or float, consisting of two, three or more logs tied
together side by side, the middle one being longer
than the others: used in East Indies, especially on
Coromandel coast, for communication with the shore.
Also – applied to similar craft used in West Indies for
short voyages and to others of much larger size used off
coast of South America; as well as kind of raft made of
two boats fastened side by side, used on St. Lawrence
and its tributaries. *Also* – an ill-natured woman. An
old kind of fire-ship long superseded. A raft with wind-
lass and grapple for recovering sunken logs.

120 Smithfield.

121 Young green cucumber used in pickling, or small kind
of cucumber used in pickling.

122 Argus.

123 A cyclops. Race of giant shepherds in Greek

mythology. Made weapons for the gods. Apollo destroyed them because they made the thunderbolts that destroyed his son.

124 United Nations Educational, Scientific and Cultural Organization.

125 Being absent without permission.

126 Ideas of magnificence without any real basis of fact.

127 There are sixty-four squares on a chess board.

128 Winds.

129 A representation of inanimate things such as fruit and vegetables.

130 The Brontës.

131 Saint Nicholas.

132 Bougainville. The plant is bougainvillea, growing mainly in South America and on Pacific isles.

Nature

133 Animals that eat dead things (carrion).

134 Part of a giant galaxy in the sky. It is made up of the sun, the planets and other heavenly bodies (asteroids) that revolve around the sun.

135 (i) They get carbon dioxide from the air. (ii) They usually draw up water through their roots. (iii) Water also brings dissolved food materials. (iv) By the process of photosynthesis the green matter in plants (chlorophyll) combines with water and carbon dioxide to form starches and sugars.

(i) Carbon dioxide plus (ii) water plus (iii) chlorophyll plus (iv) light = food (starches and sugars).

136 A horse which has a coat of white hairs mixed with hairs of a solid colour. The prevailing colour sometimes gives the prefix – black, blue or red (roan) or a mixed reddish colour.

137 The branches grow close to the trunk and point

sharply upwards. 'Fastigiate' is the term.

138 Fish need oxygen in order to live. There is some oxygen in water, but not enough to supply fish in large numbers in a limited area. The plants increase the supply, and help to keep the fish healthy. The fish give off carbon dioxide which the plants need for their own food. Plants provide a natural environment for the fish – but are not necessary in this way.

139 Male is either stag or buck; female is doe or hind.

140 Flying insects, caught on the wing.

141 The potato.

142 Flax.

143 Fish.

144 (i) Antlers are the horn-like protuberances that deer have on their heads. (ii) Anthers are end portions of the stamens (that contain the pollen) in a flower.

145 Supposed to be like a hare. Latin: *Lepus* – hare.

146 A goat. Angora goat in present usage. Historically the stuff we now call moire.

147 The palmiped is a web-footed bird.

148 The whale (Blue or sulphur-bottom whale).

149 Dam.

150 It can change colour to match its surroundings as a form of camouflage.

151 The mongoose.

152 The horse. It existed 50 million years ago. Changed through the processes of civilization. In Europe the animal (Eohippus) is called by its scientific name 'Hyracotherium', but the more picturesque synonym 'Eohippus', meaning 'dawn horse' continues in popular use.

Speed Quiz 2

153 Basket-ball.

154 Troy. Troy Weight is a standard system of weights used for gems and precious metals.

155 Friday.

156 Green.

157 Rabies.

158 Sheridan (Richard Brinsley) in *The rivals*.

159 It was the remainder of the Long Parliament.
The Long Parliament was purged in 1648 – it then became 'The Rump'.

160 Saturn.

161 Mulberry leaves.

162 Thomas Cranmer.

163 Hannibal of Carthage when he marched from Spain and crossed the Pyrenees, France and the Alps to fight the Romans in Italy.

164 Paris. The Trojan War; Menelaus was her husband.

165 White. A beginner has no grade. A kyu (next level after beginner) goes through five grades (in this order: 5, 4, 3, 2, 1) and in the same order wears belts: yellow, orange, green, blue, brown. He then becomes a dan and goes through five grades (in this order 1, 2, 3, 4, 5) and wears a red and white belt. Twelfth dan wears a white belt which is twice as wide as the beginner's belt – but this level has hardly ever been achieved.

166 William Tell.

167 Twenty years.

168 Ten.

169 A kind of tree. Monkeys find it difficult to climb.
Correct name: Chilean Pine.

170 A lizard (it has no legs).

171 Twenty-nine.

172 Gardening ... of flowers, etc. (Fellowship in this case = Membership.)

Places

173 (i) New Zealand. (ii) Wellington.
174 (i) United States of America. (ii) Washington D.C.
175 An amphitheatre in Rome.
176 The Temple of the Athena on the Acropolis, Athens.
177 Kuala Lumpur.
178 Moscow, Russia (though native of Moscow need not necessarily still live there).
179 River Seine.
180 (i) Corsica. (ii) St. Helena.
181 (i) Great Geyser. (ii) In Iceland near Reykjavik.
182 Port Said.
183 Istanbul ... and it was originally 'Byzantium'. It is a town in Turkey but is not the capital. Ankhara is the capital.
184 Adriatic Sea (on Gulf of Trieste, but at head of Adriatic.)
185 Copenhagen ... capital and largest city of Denmark.
186 Hobart.
187 An island in the Leeward Islands in the West Indies. (St Christopher.)
188 A system of stars in the sky (galaxy). A luminous 'band' of very distant stars, not separately distinguishable to the human eye. We are part of this galaxy.
189 Russia (U.S.S.R.).
190 Malta.
191 Australian.

Picture Quiz 2 – Buildings

192 Berlin: Brandenburg Gate.
193 Canberra, Australia.
194 Liverpool, England.
195 Brasilia, Brazil.
196 Sydney, Australia.
197 Quebec, Canada: Chateau Frontenac.
198 Toronto, Canada: The City Hall.
199 Venice, Italy: The Bridge of Sighs.

Team Quiz 2

200a In a desert. It is a watered spot in a desert.
200b At the mouth of a river. Tidal mouth of large river.
201a Utters sound in such a way that the voice appears to come from some other source than the speaker. Meaning literally 'speaking from the stomach'. It is the art of producing the voice without perceptible movement of the lips.
201b Someone who makes travelling arrangements, or a running messenger, one sent in haste.
202a A path fit for horse riders but not for vehicles.
202b Raised road across low or wet place or piece of water. A road formed on a 'causey' or mound, formerly also applied to a mole or landing pier running into sea or river. A highway; usually a paved way, such as existed before introduction of macadamisation ... especially Roman road, 17 century military roads, etc. In Yorkshire, causeway = pavement.
203a A class that meets for systematic study under the direction of a teacher. In German universities (hence in certain British and American universities) a select group of advanced students associated for

special study and original research under the guidance of a professor.

203b A discussion upon a single theme with an audience and important participants, and a chairman.

204a (i) A person's last achievement or production.
(ii) There is a legend that swans sing one last glorious song as they die. They do not. The mute swan, which is by far the most common swan in the U.K., is customarily silent.

204b (i) It means a straight and direct route between two places.
(ii) When bees are collecting nectar they do not move in a direct line. But when they have gathered sufficient nectar, they return to the hive by a remarkably direct route.

205a It suffered a devastating earthquake.

205b Romans destroyed it. Carthage was captured, destroyed and set on fire by the Romans in 146 B.C. after a siege that lasted two years.

206a News inserted in a paper after the printing has begun.

206b A watch with a mechanism for starting and stopping it at will. The usual purpose is to time an operation or a race, etc.

207a A grotesque and exaggerated kind of comedy, full of ludicrous incidents and expressions.

From old French *farce* = stuffing
Latin – *farcire* = to stuff

(Hence an interlude *stuffed* or inserted into the main piece).

207b Sensational dramatic play with violent appeals to the emotions, and a happy ending.

208a Pastoral Symphony.

208b The Choral Symphony.

209a We have told what we should have kept secret.

209b To act boldly whatever the risks.

210a Avoid work purposely by malingering. Correct

nautical definition – measuring the depth of the water with a lead line.

210b A job that does not lead to anything better.

211a Eat it.

211b Wear it. It is a long wrap worn by Indian women, Hindu women; also spelt saree.

212a A small donkey (also new open-sided jeep type of car).

212b Jolly Roger.

213a Milk.

213b Venison.

214a Cheese. Brie – soft, creamy cheese from C. France. Camembert – rich, soft cheese from N.W. France. Gruyère – light, Swiss cheese.

214b Tartlet . . . with pastry base and sweet filling.

215a Some china. Josiah Spode was the famous potter who invented bone china.

215b It would be furniture. George Hepplewhite, died 1786. A British furniture-maker of the 18th century who specialized in chairs. The feet of his furniture consisted of straight tapering legs that ended in spade feet. Delicately painted, carved, inlaid and decorated.

People of Long Ago

216 Duke of Cumberland.

217 Charlemagne by Pope Leo III.

218 King Alfred the Great. Once an island but now only isolated by floods.

219 Tiber.

220 When he was crossing the Wash he lost his treasure, in 1216. Crossing Cross Keys Wash near Sutton Bridge, he lost all his baggage and some of his men in crossing the river Welland. But most other authorities say John took a different route while his baggage and some of his men crossed the Wells stream (now River Nene) between Cross Keys and Long Sutton.

221 Louis with eighteen, Charles with ten.

222 Anne Hathaway.

223 King William (The Conqueror).

224 King John. It was reissued in succeeding reigns and other kings then sealed it.

225 Nero. In AD 64 he condemned Christians on the charge of setting fire to Rome.

226 Constantine. The city was renamed Constantinople at a later date.

227 King Alfred (The Great). This title was not on the manuscript. The Chronicle was probably started at the request of King Alfred and he possibly helped in the writing. Started about 892 and continued into the 12th century.

228 King Charles II. 'Here lies our sovereign Lord the King Whose word no man relies on; He never . . . . . wise one.' Written on the Bedchamber Door of Charles II.

229 King James I. (James VI of Scotland.)

230 Romulus Augustus.

231 Queen Mary I (Mary Tudor). The Bloody Tower of the Tower of London.

232 The Huguenots.

233 Genghis Khan. His real name was *Temujin* meaning 'iron smith'. He united all Mongolian tribes and established the *Yassa*, the first Mongolian code of laws.

General Knowledge 3

234 Slander is spoken defamation of character (Defamation in transient form). Libel is written and published (Defamation in a permanent form).

235 (i) A tombola is a kind of lottery with fancy articles for prizes. (Often the rotating barrel that mixes the raffle tickets.) (ii) Tombolo – a bar or spit which joins an island to the mainland or two islands.

236 Depressions, or regions where the atmospheric pressure is lower than that of its surroundings. On a weather chart the centre of a depression is usually indicated by the word 'low'.

237 First-aid device to stop bleeding. A bandage tightened by twisting with stick pressed down with screw, thus stopping blood from arteries. (Vital to know where tourniquet has to be placed and how long it is kept there – only can be done by someone with first-aid knowledge.)

238 Oath of Hippocrates. (Once repeated by medical students before they graduated as doctors.)

239 A method of bell-ringing (change-ringing) . . . Hunting through – stepping forward one pace in each succeeding row . . . Hunting back to lead – going backward one pace in each succeeding row. Instead of following in numerical sequence one bell steps forward one place in each sequence.

240 The motions of the heart (by tracing a curve on paper).

241 Yule log.

242 (i) Yellow and white/bluey-green. (ii) Sodium and mercury.

243 Catapults that directed showers of stone cannon-balls etc. against enemy fortifications.

244 Soldiers fitted their shields together to make a solid canopy and flanks to protect them when they attacked city walls. This resembled the tortoise shell, in its appearance and purpose.

245 Fine, calm weather conditions, although in winter fog is likely to develop.

246 '. . . . the shepherd's delight, but a red sky in the morning, is the shepherd's warning.'

247 A Passion Play. A play representing the sufferings and death of Jesus Christ. Oberammergau is in Bavaria, West Germany. The passion play was instigated in 1633 when the inhabitants vowed they would perform it every ten years as a token of their gratitude for deliverance from the plague.

248 Medicine. A vessel for holding liquids, especially drinks; formerly variously applied, now usually a small glass bottle, especially for liquid medicine.

249 Four years. The President must be a native-born citizen of the U.S.A. and not less than 35 years old.

250 *Tin Pan Alley* is the name given to a district occupied by composers and publishers of popular music. Refers, in England, to Denmark Street, London.

Science

251 They take place at the same time but the speed of light greatly exceeds the speed of sound.

252 (i) Calcium. (ii) Potash.

253 (i) Deuterium. (ii) Oxygen (D_2O).

254 (i) White and blue. (ii) They are both salts.

255 98·4° Fahrenheit, 36·9° Centigrade.

256 It is a form of insulation. Air is a poor conductor of heat. Therefore a layer of air between two courses of brick helps to retain the heat of the house.

257 It is believed that fluorides in minute proportions increase the resistance of teeth to dental decay.

Fluoride – a salt of hydrofluoric acid. Dental decay – dental caries.

258 The acetic acid in vinegar slows down micro-organism growth.

259 They are a source of vitamin C, essential for healthy blood vessels and sound bones and teeth. Persons who lack this vitamin may have sore gums, haemorrhage under the skin, and general fatigue.

260 Earth tremors caused by earthquakes or atomic explosions.

261 Albert Einstein . . . in 1905.

262 Heavy water.

263 Two mirrors are set so that the reflecting surfaces are exactly parallel with each other. They are arranged at an angle of 45 degrees to the axis of the tube. The light rays enter an aperture opposite one mirror and are reflected down the tube to the second mirror. This in turn sends the rays directly to the eye at the bottom aperture of the tube.

264 (i) Excellent conductor of electricity. (ii) Possesses ductility, i.e. can be drawn into thin wires without breaking. (iii) Resists corrosion.

265 Aneroid. It consists of a thin hermetically-sealed cylindric metal box, exhausted of air so that it expands and contracts with changes in the pressure of the atmosphere.

266 Altimeter. An aneroid barometer used for measuring altitude. As the plane flies higher, the atmospheric pressure is decreased and conversely.

267 Bromine (or bromide). Dark red liquid that gives off an unpleasant odour when it vaporizes.
(From Greek: *Bromos* = stink).

268 Radar – an electronic device for spotting through fog, cloud, etc.

269 The circulation of the blood. April 1616 – he gave

lectures containing the first public statement of his
thoughts on circulation.

Sport

270   The trunk of a young pine or fir tree . . . about 15 feet
in length.

271   Mick the Miller . . . the famous greyhound of the late
'twenties.

272   Darts.

273   Four.

274   Surrey.

275   (i) A boxer. (ii) London and New York.

276   It is the famous run for bobsleighs at St. Moritz in
Switzerland.

277   The University Boat Race between Oxford and
Cambridge.

278   Billiards.

279   Baseball (Also softball). Named from its shape – a 90
foot diamond. It is the infield.

280   Athletics, in the relay races. The baton is a
hollow wooden tube 'not exceeding 30 centimetres,
weight 50 grammes or more, circumference 12
centimetres'.

281   26 miles 385 yards. Standardized in 1924.

282   A student of archery.

283   Ping-pong. Name registered in 1900 in England where
it was invented by a British firm.

General Knowledge 4

284 (i) Gold. (ii) Diamonds (or gold). On the first, paper and plastics!

285 An elephant.

286 A thousand years.

287 'La Gioconda' by Leonardo da Vinci. Dates from c.1503. Now in the Louvre, Paris.

288 A leveret.

289 'Gang aft a glay' (Go often astray).

290 'Is a friend indeed'.

291 'Out of a sow's ear'.

292 The brain (Disease of the brain).

293 Britain won, France lost.

294 He works on a boat transferring goods from ship to shore. (Boat is usually flat-bottomed).

295 Carpentry joints. Tenon shaped like a dove's spread tail or reversed wedge, fitting into corresponding mortise and forming joint. Also a mortise shaped to receive such a tenon. *Dovetail moulding in architecture:* a moulding arranged in a series of figures like dovetails. *Dovetail:* To adjust exactly to form a continuous whole. To fit into each other, so as to form a compact and harmonious whole.

296 Hydrometer is an instrument for finding out specific gravity of liquids (and sometimes for finding the specific gravity of either liquids or solids). Hygrometer is an instrument for measuring humidity of air or gas (instrument used to determine the velocity or force of a current: a current-gauge).

297 He draws maps or charts.

298 Angling. *The compleat angler.* He was a merchant and an author, but he lived until he was 90 and went fishing when he was 83 years of age.

299 Painting.
300 'Dr Livingstone, I presume!'
301 Ernest Rutherford . . . of New Zealand.

Extremes

302 Halfpenny.
303 Valentina Tereshkova. Orbited the earth from 14th to 19th June, 1963. Now married to Andrian Nikolayev.
304 Greenland.
305 Mount Fuji (Fujiyama).
306 Calais. Lost by Queen Mary who was supposed to have said, 'When I die you will find Calais written on my heart.'
307 Fifteen.
308 Absolute zero.
309 Rutland.
310 Pacific. The Pacific Ocean is sometimes considered as two separate units: North and South. The South Pacific Ocean is the bigger of the two in area, and is still the biggest ocean in the world.
311 The humming-bird. The bee humming-bird of Cuba is less than 2 inches long.
312 A dog. The first live creature ever to circle the earth in a satellite. On November 3, 1957, in Sputnik II. She subsequently came back to earth safely.
313 An atomic power plant. It was the world's first atomic power station (to serve the public). Opened by the Queen on October 17, 1956. In Cumberland, Windscale.
314 Ben Nevis. 4,406 feet. Biggest in British Isles.
315 (i) Palm Sunday. (ii) Easter Sunday.
316 Genesis (the beginning).
317 Revelation.
318 Andorra in the Pyrenees Mountains. Andorra comprises a group of valleys in the Central Pyrenees. An annual

payment is made to the officials; about £1 to the President and £4 with six hams, six cheeses and twelve hens to the bishop.

319   (i) San Marino. (ii) Italy. One 'regent captain' represents the city, and one the rural district. Also believed to be Europe's oldest republic.

Games and Sport

320   Queensberry Rules.

321   Ski-ing.

322   Le Mans. The Le Mans 24 Hour Race has been held annually since 1923 – except in 1936 and from 1940 to 1948 when no races were held.

323   16 pounds.

324   January 1.

325   A serve that is too good to be returned.

326   A race in which all runners start from the same mark. There is no handicap.

327   Mountaineering. Crampons are the plates set with iron spikes which can be fastened to the soles of the boots to hold on icy surfaces. Pitons are the pegs that are stuck into rock cracks or into ice.

328   Archery. Bracers are the guards that are worn on the lower part of the arm that holds the bow. Quivers are the containers in which the arrows are carried.

329   Figure Eight. Variations are based on this figure. There are sixty-nine possible combinations of figures.

330   Nine (on each side).

331   Twelve, i.e. each player has twelve men.

332   Sixteen. Each player has eight pawns, two knights, two bishops, two rooks, one queen and one king.

333   In cricket it is a ball which pitches directly underneath the bat.

334 A hand of cards with not one of them above 9. In bridge or whist.

335 Five. There are three matches in which six teams take part. In the next round there will be four matches with eight teams taking part.

336 The wind strength must not exceed 4·47 miles per hour or 2 metres (or 6 ft. 6 in. per second).

337 Sidney Barnes. Taken out of League cricket in 1901 to tour Australia and in his first two tests in Australia he took 19 wickets. During his career he took 189 Test wickets. Born at Smethwick, Staffs, in 1873.

Picture Quiz 3 – Tools and Instruments

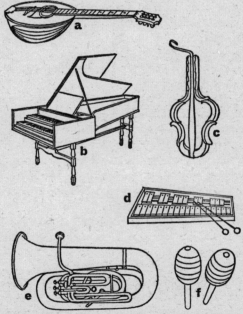

338 (a) Mandoline. (b) Harpsichord. (c) Jew's Harp. (d) Glockenspiel. (e) Tuba. (f) Marracas.

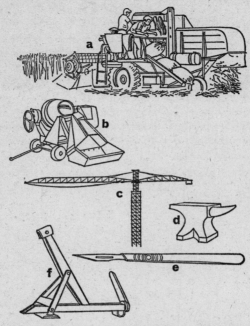

339 (a) Combine harvester. (b) Cement mixer. (c) Crane.
(d) Anvil. (e) Scalpel. (f) Car jack.

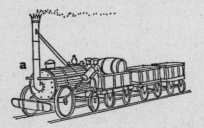

340 (a) This is the *Rocket* which was constructed by the
Stephensons to take part in the Rainhill Trials. It is

regarded as the first commercially successful locomotive,
partly due to the introduction of a new heating system.
(b) Jethro Tull's drill. This drill bored straight rows of
holes into which seed was dropped. It was the first
machine used for this purpose. (c) Hargreaves' Spinning
Jenny. The first machine to spin many threads at a
time. The spindles of several spinning wheels were placed
upright and in a row. A frame was added from which
threads were made. The Jenny was patented in 1770.
The name is probably derived from 'engine'.

Team Quiz 3

341a   Rowing.

341b   Boxing.

342a   Baseball.

342b   Wrestling.

343a   Cricket.

343b   Poker.

344a   The President of the United States.

344b   In the blood.

345a   Larboard (port).

345b   Fore part.

346a   The didjeridoo is a musical instrument played by aborigines. Made from straight, hollowed-out pieces of wood, usually more than 6 ft. long. Belongs to the trumpet family. The didjeridoo is played at religious ceremonies.

346b   Bag used especially by Australian travellers in the bush to hold food.

347a   Because you would have found exactly the right word.

347b   Copying out the notes word for word.

348a   The Koran. Consists of Mohammed's sayings.

348b   Japan.

349a   A parallelogram. A rectangle, rhombus and a square are all parallelograms, as they each possess the properties of a parallelogram.

349b   An isosceles triangle.

350a   A toastmaster. He would be announcing a speaker or a 'Toast to be drunk' at a dinner or banquet.

350b   Parliament (House of Commons). The phrase is used by an M.P. to draw the Speaker's attention to unauthorized people in the House.

351a   *Honi soit qui mal y pense.* (Evil be to him who evil thinks.)

351b   *Post Scriptum* (addition to letter).

352a A mongoose.

352b He was the pig who bullied, tortured and killed other creatures into submission or persuaded them to follow his rebellious lead. They won and Manor Farm became Animal Farm with Napoleon king over all. Napoleon was a 'Berkshire Boar'.

353a *Born free* (by Joy Adamson).

353b *Wind in the willows* (by Kenneth Grahame).

354a It burns with a brilliant white light. Also used with colour in fireworks to make them extra brilliant.

354b It burns with a crimson red flare. This is the reason it is used in railway signal flares and distress rockets.

355a A person given to gossip (iii). Also a member of a Cambridge University Cricket Club.

355b Sentence construction (iii).

356a Peeping Tom . . . who looked out when Godiva passed along the street in Coventry, and was struck blind.

356b Tom, Tom, the piper's son . . . stole a pig and away did run.

General Knowledge 5

357 Medicine.

358 Journalism.

359 They were brothers. Charles II 1660–85, James II 1685–89.

360 King Edward II (1314).

361 We cry . . . they are our tear glands in the eye.

362 You would be well away from the ground on the back of an elephant. A 'howdah' is a seat for two or more persons riding on the back of an elephant. Usually has a canopy. Can also be applied to a seat on a camel.

363 Africa. N.W. They extend from Cape Nun on the Atlantic Ocean through Morocco, Algeria and

Tunisia to the Gulf of Cabes on the Mediterranean Sea. Comprises of Anti-Atlas, Sahara Atlas and the Great Atlas ranges.

364 Isles of Scilly or Scilly Islands. About 140 islands altogether about 25 miles from Land's End in Cornwall. Only five are inhabited, the other two being St Agnes and St Martins.

365 Orkney Islands. About seventy islands altogether of which twenty-six are inhabited. Others include North and South Ronaldsay, Burray, Rousay, Shapinsay, Stronsay, Edray, Westray and Sanday. North of the British Isles and separated from the mainland by the Pentland Firth which is $6\frac{1}{2}$ miles wide.

366 He would vote.

367 An apple ... a medium-sized good eating apple with good flesh.

368 Russia (Government officials).

369 The time it takes for the moon to orbit the earth. Interval from new moon – new moon or full moon – full moon. Scientists measure the revolution round the earth in synodic and sidereal months. Synodic month (which is the one that is commonly known as the 'lunar month') is the period from one new moon to another, i.e. the time taken for the moon to revolve around the earth and return to its original position in relation to the sun. The moon completes one revolution round the earth in 29 days 12 hrs. 44 mins. 3 secs. The sidereal month measures the moon's revolution in relation to a fixed star (about $27\frac{1}{2}$ days). The difficulty in constructing a calendar arises from the lunation not containing an exact number of days; the year not containing an exact number of lunations – 12 lunations = 354 days.

370 January. Named after Janus, who was also the Roman God of 'beginnings'. Presided over the entrance to the year. Represented with two faces, one looking forward

and one backward. Shown with keys and staff.

371 Cereal. Ceres was the goddess. The Greeks called her Demeter. She was the protectress of agriculture and of all the fruits of the earth. Mother of Persephone (Proserpina in Roman mythology).

372 Narcissus. He was the son of the river god Cephisus. The nymph Echo pined away and died because of his neglect. As a punishment, the gods made him fall in love with his own reflection in a pool of clear water. At last he died and was changed into the flower *narcissus*. Other versions include Ovid – saying he died of unrequited love and was changed into the flower called poet's narcissus. Another version says the flower sprang from the blood when he killed himself. It is possible that the legend is connected with the ancient superstition that it was unlucky to see one's own reflection.

Quotations

373 King Charles II . . . on his deathbed, 1685, of Nell Gwynne.

374 Queen Elizabeth I . . . 'and a king of England too' at Tilbury in 1588, on the approach of the Armada.

375 (i) *Elegy in a country churchyard* (by Thomas Gray).
     (ii) 'Far from the madding crowd's ignoble strife
          Their sober wishes never learn'd to stray:
          Along the cool sequestered vale of life
          They kept the noiseless tenor of their way.'

376 (i) Ernest Hemingway. (ii) John Donne.

377 *Hamlet* . . . by Shakespeare.

378 (i) (Edith Louisa) Nurse Cavell. (ii) Before her execution by the Germans in the First World War. She was in charge of a Brussels hospital during occupation. She helped allied soldiers (200) to escape. Sentenced to death

by German court-martial, she was executed by firing squad.

379 (i) Winston Churchill. (ii) When the pilots of Britain's air squadrons were beating back the invading German bombers during the Battle of Britain, 1940.

380 *The Charge of the Light Brigade*. Written in memory of the charge of Lord Cardigan's Light Brigade during the Crimean War.

381 *Morte d'Arthur*.

382 'Four Larks and a Wren
Have all built their nests in my beard.'

383 (i) 'Anon! Anon!' (ii) Boar's Head. In Shakespeare's *Henry IV part 2*.

384 *Alice's adventures in Wonderland* by Lewis Carroll.

385 The skylark (in 'To a skylark').

386 (i) Samuel Pepys (in his diary). (ii) Nell Gwynne who became the mistress of King Charles II.

387 24,902 miles – 24,901·8 to be exact, English – but allow any number between 24 thousand and 26 thousand.

388 30 feet (One fathom is 6 feet). In *The tempest*.

389 The mutineers singing round their camp fire in *Treasure Island* by Robert Louis Stevenson.

390 (i) *On his blindness*. (ii) John Milton.

391 (i) *Tale of two cities*. (ii) Charles Dickens.

392 (i) *Pride and prejudice*. (ii) Jane Austen.

Speed Quiz 3

393 Source.
394 A Londoner. A person born within hearing of Bow Bells.
395 Tweedledum.
396 The Irish Sea.
397 Goose.
398 The Little Mermaid. From a fairy-tale by Hans Christian Andersen.
399 Prague. In centre of city. Prague was ruled by the Duke of Bohemia in the 10th Century – he was known as King Wenceslaus I or 'Good King Wenceslaus'.
400 Thumb or finger. Bone between knuckle and first joint. Not to be confused with metatarsal, relating to bones between tarsus and toes.
401 Columbine.
402 William Blake.
403 Three. *The three sisters.*
404 Primates.
405 In Milan, Italy. On the site of the Church of Santa Maria Della Scala.
406 Kon-tiki.
407 Harmonica or mouth organ.
408 Chromium. Stainless steel contains at least 10% chromium. Ordinary stainless steel such as knives and forks contain 18% chromium and 8% nickel.
409 River Zambezi. David Livingstone first discovered and described the falls in 1855.
410 Four.
411 In the body (more correctly, in the pancreas).

Here and There

412 Morocco.

413 Taj Mahal. At Agra, India.

414 Yugoslavia. Born 1892. President of Yugoslavia since 1953.

415 Spain. Born 1892. In 1935, Francisco Franco became Chief of Army General Staff and in 1936 led a revolt against the Republican Government. In 1937, Franco proclaimed himself *El Caudillo* (the leader). In 1939 when Spanish Civil War ended, he became Prime Minister. In 1947 he was declared Chief of State for life.

416 Fifty.

417 He would be suggesting that you had powers of persuasion to get what you wanted. The Blarney Stone is in Blarney Castle in Ireland. A former owner persuaded besiegers to delay plundering the castle and this gave the name of the castle and stone to the vocabulary.

418 Balearic Islands.

419 Il Duce (the leader).

420 The Métropolitain or more commonly just the 'Métro'.

421 (i) Pacific Ocean. (ii) They are named after James Cook, the explorer, who charted them.

422 Egyptians.

423 Potato crop . . . 1845–7.

424 Hawaii. Accept 'Honolulu' although that is actually a town on Hawaii. They are dancing girls.

425 49°. (Sometimes referred to as the 49th Parallel.)

426 Ecuador. (The equator crosses the country and Ecuador is the Spanish for equator.)

427 Fort Knox.

428 The Great Trek was the migration of the Boers in Southern Africa. Late 1830s. When the British took

control of the Cape Colony in Africa in 1806. The Boers
(Dutch farmers) travelled into the Southern Africa
interior. They founded Orange Free State, Transvaal
and Natal.

Picture Quiz 4 – Costume
429   Shako.
430   Mantilla. Spanish girls.
431   Sporran.
432   Siamese dancers.
433   Farthingale.
434   Hennin.
435   Chlamys.

Team Quiz 4
436a Sword (or bayonet). Scabbard – the case or sheath
      which serves to protect the blade of a sword, dagger or
      bayonet when not in use.
436b Arrows.
437a President of the French Republic.
437b The Archbishop of Canterbury.
438a Fish (Potatoes are also possible, lobsters, etc). It is a
      fisherman's wicker basket.
438b Furniture. It can be either a van or a depository.
439a A vet. (or veterinary surgeon).
439b A poacher.
440a A nickname thought to be originally given to an
      inhabitant of New England in the United States by the
      New Yorkers; an inhabitant of the Northern States
      as distinguished from a Southerner and now frequently
      used to describe all citizens of the U.S.A.
440b The name given to a long-haired humped grunting
      animal of Tibet.

441a Water boils at this heat.

441b It is the boiling point of water.

442a Tuesday. The day before Ash Wednesday, the beginning of Lent. There is a famous pancake day race at Olney, in England, at which each competitor must toss her pancake three times during the race.

442b Thursday . . . exactly forty days after Easter.

443a The deadly nightshade. *Atropa belladonna.*

443b The foxglove.

444a Suez Canal.

444b Panama Canal.

445a She was turned into a 'pillar of salt'. Genesis 13, verse 19.

445b He or she was turned into stone. Medusa was one of the three Gorgons. The hair on her head was composed of snakes. Perseus cut off her head.

446a A four-poster is a bed with four posts at the corners for supporting a canopy or curtains. It gave privacy, and even more important in the days before central heating, it kept out the draughts.

446b A carriage with four horses driven by one person. The question has been 'tied down' by the word 'Victorian', but the expression can also be used to describe a necktie, tied in a slipknot with the ends hanging vertically.

447a A 'four-pounder' was a gun that shot a projectile weighing four pounds.

447b The fourth of July is celebrated as Independence Day. Declaration of Independence on July 4, 1776.

448a (i) Soprano. (ii) Contralto. (iii) Tenor. (iv) Bass.

448b (i) Spades. (2) Clubs. (3) Hearts. (iv) Diamonds. Each suit has thirteen cards.

449a The ostrich. To bury one's head in the sand is to avoid the obvious because one does not wish to believe it.

449b The crocodile. When people are accused of shedding 'crocodile tears' they are supposed to be insincere in their grief.

450a Wall Street. Apart from the Stock Exchange it contains many great commercial houses and banks, and is considered the heart of US financial affairs.

450b Bourse.

451a Mayflower.

451b Santa Maria. The ship was wrecked later in the voyage and Columbus returned in the Nina.

Who am I?

452 Kwama Nkrumah.

453 Leon Trotsky.

454 Dr. Edward Jenner.

455 Benjamin Franklin.

456 Jonathan Swift.

457 Robert Louis Stevenson.

458 King Henry VIII.

459 William Shakespeare.

460 Sir Ernest Shackleton.

461 Mary, Queen of Scots. In fact Elizabeth I and Mary, Queen of Scots were second cousins. Elizabeth signed the death warrant.

462 Tennessee Williams (Thomas Lanier Williams).

463 Sir Thomas Lipton.

464 Ringo Starr.

465 Giuseppe Garibaldi.

466 Sir Walter Scott.

467 Thomas Alva Edison.

468 Queen Elizabeth I of England.

469 Joan Sutherland.

470 Sir Walter Raleigh.

471 Sean O'Casey.

The Bible

472 The first five books of the Old Testament of the Bible (Genesis, Exodus, Leviticus, Numbers and Deuteronomy).

473 Mount Ararat. In Turkey near the border with Iran and USSR.

474 Joseph.

475 Daniel.

476 Jairus's.

477 Delilah betrayed Samson.

478 (i) Caspar. (ii) Melchior. (iii) Balthazar.

479 (i) Caspar brought frankincense. (ii) Melchior brought gold. (iii) Balthazar brought myrrh.

480 Moses.

481 Samuel.

482 Wisdom.

483 Psalms. Approximately 73 of the 150 psalms are generally attributed to David. Other authors include Moses and Solomon. The psalms are sacred poems and were intended to be sung.

484 Parables. E.g. The good samaritan, The lost sheep, etc. Fictitious stories to illustrate spiritual and moral things.

485 Mount Sinai.

486 (i) Sling or catapult and pebble or stone. (ii) Harp.

487 Angels. Cherubims or cherubs often illustrated as winged children.

488 Saint Paul. Galatia was an ancient kingdom located in Asia Minor (the *exact* location is in dispute). The letters are known as *The Epistle to the Galatians*.

489 Absalom was killed by Joab.

490 Salome. Daughter of Herodias. Not mentioned by name in the New Testament. Danced before Herod Antipas and this was a reward for her dancing.

Speed Quiz 4

491 Hungary.

492 Ecuador.

493 Iceland.

494 Bulgaria.

495 Chile.

496 Latvia.

497 Tunisia.

498 Ethiopia.

499 Dr Samuel Johnson and James Boswell. Tom Davies was the bookseller with a bookshop at No. 8 Russell Street, Covent Garden.

500 Mermaid Tavern.

501 (i) Malaysia (or Malaya – old name). (ii) Ethiopia. Tunku Abdul Rahman is the prime minister (and Minister of Foreign Affairs) of Malaysia (Tunku is his title). Haile Selassie is Emperor of Ethiopia and the Lion of Judah is one of his titles.

502 Brandenburg Gate.

503 Hanseatic League.

504 Adonais.

505 Thomas de Quincey.

506 Pogroms.

507 Bleaching powder.

508 On the bottom of a boat. The backbone of a ship. It runs along the lowest part of the hull from bow to stern.

509 Population explosion.

510 The witch of Endor.

General Knowledge 6

511   The Maquis.

512   Spelling the word as it was sounded.

513   For forty days and forty nights.

514   Verdigris.

515   The Maelstrom . . . caused by the current which flows
       between two of the Lofoten Islands.

516   The Gestapo was the Secret Police force of Nazi
       Germany.

517   The lark.

518   (i) Infra-red rays. (ii) Ultra-violet rays.

519   Michelangelo.

520   A rainbow in the sky. The title of this poem is
       'My heart leaps up'.

521   Prussic acid or hydrocyanic acid.

522   Brazil.

523   A form of bubonic plague. To be even more specific
       caused by a germ *Pasteurella pestis*, bringing *buboes*,
       which were swellings of the lymph glands.

524   A dog (toy). Possibly imported to Mexico from China
       during the late 1500s. Almost entirely hairless and very
       small.

525   Linseed oil. The flax seeds contain the oil which
       is used in the manufacture of paints, varnishes, linoleum
       and oil-cloth.

526   (i) spontaneous applause.

527   (i) a kind of bread . . . made from coarse ground rye.

528   Winston Churchill. In the Canadian Senate and in
       House of Commons, December 30, 1941.

529   The Jackdaw of Rheims. One of the best-known of
       Barham's *Ingoldsby Legends*; tells of a jackdaw which
       stole the ring of the Archbishop of Rheims.

530   Coins. Numismatists collect coins. Nobles were

English gold coins instituted by Edward III and issued down to the reign of Henry VII.

Literature 2

531 Elizabeth Barrett.

532 Gladys Aylward. The film *The Inn of the Sixth Happiness* was also based on her life. She spent twenty years in China.

533 A masque. A dramatic presentation with music, and emphasis on the visual. An entertainment in which fine costumes, scenery, music and dancing are more important than the story. So named because the performers originally wore masks. *Comus* was first presented at Ludlow Castle in 1634 on Michaelmas Night (September 29).

534 Captain W. E. Johns. He died in 1968.

535 George Eliot. Pseudonym of Mary Ann Evans, born at Arbury, went to school at 29 Warwick Row, Coventry, taught by the Misses Franklin.

536 Jerome K. Jerome. Born at Walsall in 1859 (middle name Klapka).

537 (i) Bean sticks or beanstalks. (The beans he planted and grew.)
(ii) The hen that laid the golden eggs, a golden harp and a bag of gold.

538 Canterbury. By T. S. Eliot (Archbishop Thomas Becket was murdered).

539 *The Arabian Nights* or, more properly, *A thousand and one nights*. According to legend King Shahryar (King in the islands of India and China) killed all his wives. He spared Scheherazade's life as long as she entertained him with a tale each night. In the end he spared her life altogether.

540 John Milton.

541   Douglas Bader (Group Captain), C.B.E., D.S.O., D.F.C. Lost both legs in a flying accident in 1931. Rejoined R.A.F. in 1939 and was captured after collision with German aircraft in 1941.

542   Tabard. The Prologue to the *Canterbury Tales* – 'In Southwark at The Tabard as I lay ready to wenden on my pilgrimage to Canterbury with full devout courage.'

543   H. G. Wells. Written in 1901. First of Wells' works to be filmed. Wrote many other science fiction books including *The time machine* and *The war of the worlds*.

544   He gave him the gift that everything he touched turned to gold. This was because Midas had helped Silenus, the teacher of Dionysus (or Bacchus). The power became a curse as even his food turned to gold. Dionysus told him to bathe in the River Pactolus, and the magic left him. But the sands became golden.

545   D'Artagnan . . . in *The three musketeers* by Alexander Dumas.

Team Quiz 5

546a   Australia.

546b   China. Also Japan, Korea.

547a   Russia. It is a Russian tea-urn.

547b   Finland.

548a   France (Headquarters originally in Algeria but now in Corsica). Spain also have a smaller, less well-known Foreign Legion working on the same principles.

548b   Greece. Ancient Greek battle formation.

549a   Tokyo. Yen currency also used in Japanese possessions.

549b   Moscow. Gum – Gosudarstvenny Universalny Magazin (State Department Store in the Red Square. Tourists shop here to take advantage of the special facilities).

550a   Pig (or swine).

550b   Sheep.

551a	Eagle.
551b	Wolf.
552a	Lion.
552b	Cow or bull or ox.
553a	River Danube.
553b	St Lawrence. Montreal lies on the triangular island of Montreal in southern Quebec.
554a	Army officer.
554b	Girls who work in a domestic capacity in a foreign home with agreed privileges in order to learn the language and more about the country.
555a	Cardinal Richelieu.
555b	Bismarck.
556a	Napoleon's. A hospital for veteran soldiers.
556b	Lenin's.
557a	Egypt. Workers on the land.
557b	Italy. Soldiers trained for mountain warfare.
558a	A toastmaster is a person who announces the speakers at a public dinner or banquet.
558b	You would be running away as fast as you could.
559a	A steeplejack. Could be spidermen with metal construction.
559b	Plastic surgeon.
560a	Humpty Dumpty.
560b	Jack (Jack and Jill).
561a	On the summits of the Himalayas in Tibet. The Yeti, legendary monster whose footprints have been seen.
561b	At the bottom of the sea. The 'watery grave of sailors'. Davy Jones is sometimes referred to as the spirit of the seas.

Picture Quiz 5 – Birds and Animals

562 Duck-billed platypus. (Australia.)
563 Beaver. Lodge. (American continent.)
564 Pelican.
565 Ants. It is the giant ant-eater.
566 Armadillo.
567 Swift.
568 Bower bird. It builds a bower for its intended mate. (Australia)
569 Lyre bird. (Australia)
570 A mammal. A bat.

General Knowledge 7

571 The Church or religion. In 16th century. Dispute between Rome and the various national churches of Europe. The reformation led to the establishment of Protestantism. Led by Martin Luther; the nailing of his thesis in Wittenburg in 1517 is generally taken as the opening date of the Reformation.
572 If your hearing was all right. An audiometer measures the acuteness of hearing.
573 The intensity of light. Also a device for determining the proper duration of exposure in photography.
574 A clerestory is the upper part of the nave, choir and transepts of a church, containing a series of windows, clear of the roofs of the side aisles, admitting light to the central part of the building. From *clear-story window* – in Roman times, many great halls were lighted in this way.
575 Peru. Central Railway of Peru between Callao and Lroya.
576 The Mont Blanc tunnel in the Alps connecting France and Italy.

577 The heavens/globe/world.

578 Rebirth. From the French *renaître* – to be born again.
The Renaissance began in Italy in the 14th Century and
it was a great revival of art and literature.

579 Castle or fortress. Strong heavy grating sliding up and
down in vertical grooves at sides of gateway. Acts as
part of the fortifications to prevent people entering or
leaving without authority.

580 There was a plot to blow up the king and the Houses of
Parliament. The searchers discovered a group of people
including Guy Fawkes in the cellars with the gunpowder
and were able to prevent the catastrophe.

581 Greek soldiers were hidden in the horse. After the gates
of the city were closed at night they crept out, opened
the gates and let the Greek army in. The city was
plundered and burnt.

582 The Salic Law excludes female succession to the throne.
William IV, who reigned before Victoria, was king of
Hanover as well as king of the United Kingdom of
Great Britain and Ireland. But according to
Hanoverian Salic Law the kingdom passed to an uncle
of Victoria, the Duke of Cumberland. The Salic Law
is still in force in Belgium, Liechtenstein, Norway and
Sweden.

583 Silicon transistors are less sensitive to changes in
temperature than are germanium transistors.

584 A gas that will not combine readily with any other
chemical element. A gas which is chemically inactive.
Also krypton, xenon, neon and radon. Also does not
easily burn, or support combustion.

585 A composition of two or more metals, or metal plus
non-metallic substance. Pewter is mainly tin but other
metals are added to get the required characteristics.
Other metals used with pewter are copper, lead,
antimony and occasionally bismuth. Bronze consists of

copper and tin. Phosphorus, lead, zinc, aluminium and silicon may be added. Originally 'alloy' was used when a base metal was mixed with a 'nobler' one, especially in connection with coinage of gold and silver.

586 A shadow . . . cast by the gnomon, which is the name given to the flat piece of metal (or rod) sticking up from the centre of the dial. The position or length of the shadow indicates the hour.

587 An air bubble . . . which has been left in the liquid that fills the glass tube otherwise (alcohol or ether) and which moves when the spirit level is tilted. A spirit level is used for finding a horizontal line or plane.

Master Brain

588 (i) Battle of Waterloo (1815). (ii) Napoleon rode Marengo: Wellington rode Copenhagen.

589 The point at which the sun appears to be farthest from the Equator. Solstice: one or other of two times in the year, midway between the two equinoxes, when the sun having reached the tropical points is farthest from the Equator and appears to stand still, i.e. June 21, December 22. The winter sun of the northern hemisphere and summer sun of the southern.

590 It was the beginning of the Trades Union Movement. It was the home of six farm workers who banded together to get an increase in wages. They were sentenced to seven years transportation and became known as the Tolpuddle Martyrs (1834). (They were not charged for forming a trade union, but for administering unlawful oaths in connection with it.)

591 Brussels (Belgium): Amsterdam (Netherlands or Holland): Bonn (Federal or West Germany): Paris (France): Luxembourg (Luxembourg): Rome (Italy).

592 7,926·5 miles.

593 24,901·8 miles.

594 (1) 100 metres   (6) 110 metres hurdles
    (2) Long jump   (7) Discus throw
    (3) Shot put   (8) Pole vault
    (4) High jump   (9) Javelin throw
    (5) 400 metres   (10) 1,500 metres
        (first day)   (second day)

595 It was built as a temple to honour all their gods.
The name means *of all the gods,* and this name was
given to any temple which served the purpose of
worship of all the gods. Agrippa built the one in
the centre of Rome in 27 B.C.

596 Six. New South Wales, Victoria, South Australia,
Queensland, Tasmania, Western Australia. Australia
Capital Territory and Northern Territory are not states.

597 (1) Hanley. (2) Burslem. (3) Tunstall. (4) Stoke-upon-
Trent. (5) Longton.

598 Pauli Exclusion principle. The Austrian theoretical
physicist, Wolfgang Pauli, won the 1945 Nobel prize in
physics for this discovery.

599 The clockwork model of the planetary system. Named
after Earl of Orrery (1676–1731). English Statesman for
whom an early copy of the machine was made.

600 Java Man. Scientifically *Homo erectus javensis.*

601 Aries, Taurus, Gemini, Cancer, Leo, Virgo, Libra,
Scorpio, Sagittarius, Capricorn, Aquarius, Pisces.

602 (Juan Sebastian Del) Cano.

603 (i) Metamorphic. (ii) Igneus.

Meeting Places

604   Waterloo. Battle of Waterloo June 17–19, 1815.
Act of Congress of Vienna June 9, 1815.

605   Athens.

606   Moscow.

607   In a railway coach. Forest of Compiègne in France at
5 a.m., November 11, 1918. Hostilities ceased at 11 a.m.
on the Western Front.

608   On board a battleship, *Missouri*, in Tokyo Bay on
September 2, 1945.

609   In a farmhouse (at Appomattox Court House,
Virginia.)

610   Kaaba. Mohammed, the founder of the Islamic
religion, was born in Mecca, in Saudi Arabia. The
Great Mosque is the centre of worship for Moslems.
A small stone building known as the Kaaba is in the
centre of an open area within the mosque. On the
south wall rests the Black Stone enclosed in a silver
ring. Moslems face the Kaaba and the Black Stone when
they pray. The Black Stone, according to the Moslem
tradition, was given to Abraham by the angel Gabriel.

611   Chinese.

612   Canada. Yukon in N.W. Canada. Mine takes its name
from the Kimberley River.

613   Madame Tussaud. Swiss modeller in wax born in 1760.
In 1794 married François Tussaud. Brought collection
to England and after successful show at the Lyceum
Theatre, toured the country with it. Exhibition
established in Baker Street, London in 1833.

614   Celestial City.

615   (i) Belgium. (ii) The Netherlands (Holland). (iii)
Luxembourg. It came into operation in 1948.

616   To the Never-Never Land.

617 Lord Chancellor.

618 This is the room where monks have their meals. The word is used generally for refectory tables, refectory room at college etc., but always with the same utility meaning.

619 In Washington D.C., United States. North Atlantic Treaty Organization, 4 April 1949.

Picture Quiz 6 – Music

620 (a) 'Auld Lang Syne'

(b) 'Frère Jacques'

(c) 'Waltzing Matilda'

Composer—Marie Cowan. This music is printed by kind permission of Allans Music (Australia) Pty Ltd and Oxford University Press.

(d) 'John Brown's Body' or 'The Battle Hymn'.

General Knowledge 8

621 Purl.

622 Cheeses.

623 Help you to smell. The nose is the main olfactory organ.

624 A body. Stone coffin . . . Egyptians, Greeks and Romans.

625 The five continents of the world.

626 Turkey.

627 Truth.

628 (i) Which was to be demonstrated or proved. (ii) The abbreviation 'Q.E.D.' is used when a geometrical theorem is proved.

629 (i) Those who are about to die salute you. (ii) This phrase was shouted by Roman gladiators as they entered the arena ready to do combat for life or death.

630 Rosetta Stone. Discovered in the mud near the mouth (Rosetta) of the Nile by a French Officer in 1799. On the stone is carved a decree of Ptolemy V Epiphanes. Three inscriptions (i) in ancient Egyptian hieroglyphics. (ii) in Demotic. (iii) In Greek. Through Jean Francois Champiollion solved the riddle of the language of Ancient Greece. Now in British Museum.

631 Greenwich.

632 Sappho. Lived about 600 B.C. at Mitylene on the island of Lesbos.

633 $E = mc^2$ (Energy equals mass times the velocity of light squared).

634 Proton.

635 Strontium–90.

Among the famous titles available in Knight Books are

J M Barrie
PETER PAN AND WENDY

Enid Blyton
FIVE ON A TREASURE ISLAND

Pamela Brown
THE SWISH OF THE CURTAIN

Captain W E Johns
BIGGLES IN THE BLUE

Stanley Phillips
STAMP COLLECTING

Mary Treadgold
THE HERON RIDE

Jean Webster
DADDY-LONG-LEGS

E̶... ...i̶t̶e̶d̶ a dark eyebrow. "Be gentle with me," he said mockingly. **Closing his eyes, he propped his chin on his folded arms and waited for me to touch him.**

Touch him.

I looked down at my hands, which felt suddenly tingly. I knew how to give a professional massage. Why were my hands shaking? I didn't feel like a competent physical therapist. I felt like what he'd once called me—a frightened virgin.

Edward St. Cyr, my boss, who'd inspired me and irritated me in equal measure, who was way out of my league and didn't see me as anything more than someone he could casually flirt with, perhaps casually sleep with and casually forget, was naked beneath my hands. And I feared if I showed a moment of weakness he might roll over and devour me.

If he felt my hands shaking... All he had to do was turn around on the table and pull me down hard against him in a savage kiss.

Don't think about it, I told myself fiercely.

Flexing my fingers, I poured oil in one palm, then rubbed my hands together to warm them. Slowly, I lowered them to his skin.

As I ran my hands down the trapezius muscles of his upper back I tried to calm the rapid beat of my heart. But as I stroked and rubbed Edward beneath my palms I felt hot as summer. I closed my eyes, trying *not* to imagine what it would be like if he were my lover. How it would feel to sink into the pleasure I imagined he'd give me.

Afterward my soul might be ash, but I'd finally know the exhilaration of the fire.

Jennie Lucas grew up dreaming about faraway lands. At fifteen, hungry for experience beyond the borders of her small Idaho city, she went to a Connecticut boarding school on scholarship. She took her first solo trip to Europe at sixteen, then put off college and travelled around the US, supporting herself with jobs as diverse as gas station cashier and newspaper advertising assistant.

At twenty-two she met the man who would be her husband. After their marriage she graduated from Kent State with a degree in English. Seven years after she started writing she got the magical call from London that turned her into a published author.

Since then life has been hectic, with a new writing career, a sexy husband and two small children, but she's having a wonderful (albeit sleepless) time. She loves immersing herself in dramatic, glamorous, passionate stories. Maybe she can't physically travel to Morocco or Spain right now, but for a few hours a day, while her children are sleeping, she can be there in her books.

Jennie loves to hear from her readers. You can visit her website at www.jennielucas.com, or drop her a note at jennie@jennielucas.com

Recent titles by the same author:

UNCOVERING HER NINE MONTH SECRET
THE SHEIKH'S LAST SEDUCTION
THE CONSEQUENCES OF THAT NIGHT
   (At His Service)
A REPUTATION FOR REVENGE
   (Princes Untamed)